THE FLOWER BOOK

THE FLOWER BOOK

Contents

Foreword

I consider myself one of the lucky few who get to do what they love for a living. Arranging the flowers I have worked so hard to grow is, for me, the ultimate expression of creativity. In this book I want to share with you how I create my natural-style arrangements.

I chanced upon this career after some years of working in horticulture. My last job brought me to a walled kitchen garden where I was employed to grow produce, including flowers, for the big house. I was able to grow and forage whatever I liked in order to create arrangements inspired by this quintessentially English location. After six years of experimentation and learning, I took the leap and set up my own flower farm, Green and Gorgeous, in the Oxfordshire countryside. At the farm, we offer a local, seasonal, and natural alternative to more commercial suppliers. I have no formal training and do not claim to be a florist. My style is intuitive and soulful, guided by how plants grow and interact with each other in the garden and in nature. This leads to arrangements that are airy and abundant, with plenty of space for pollinators to wing their way between the stems. I consider my work to be an expression of my love for flowers.

The opening chapter of this book works through my arrangement process step by step. I start with the container, considering the size, shape, and material. The next stage is selecting my palette of flowers and foliage. I always work with what is in season as this helps to narrow down the overwhelming range that is available. What is more, this practice provides immediate examples of natural combinations as flowers that are in season at the same time tend to look more at ease with each other.

I break down the arrangement process itself into three stages, which I refer to as the three "F"s: "foliage", "focal flowers", and "final flourish". I will expand on each stage, showing how they help me to create all of my arrangements. I have also included more specific notes on the principles of arranging front-facing displays and centrepieces, as well as illustrated, step-by-step instructions on how to create a hand-tied bouquet.

I like to create arrangements with plenty of space for pollinators to wing their way between the stems.

The main section of the book has sixty profiles of my favourite cut flowers divided into chapters by season. Each profile contains information on why the bloom makes a good cut flower, how it is best displayed, and what to look for when buying or harvesting stems. Accompanying half of the profiles are step-by-step arrangement recipes that illustrate one of the ways in which I feel these flowers are best displayed.

I hope you enjoy this book, and that it inspires you to seek out and arrange seasonal flowers, perhaps locally, or even to grow some in your own garden.

Rachel Siegfried

DESIGNING WITH FLOWERS

Choose a Container

For me, every arrangement starts with the container, so this should be your first consideration. Think about what mood or style you want to evoke, and the flowers that may be available to you. Here are examples of different types of containers and which types of flowers work well in them. Remember, anything can be a container as long as it can be made watertight.

MUGS & JUGS
I love the simplicity of glazed ceramic mugs or jugs. They come in an endless variety of shapes and colours, and their domestic nature works well with a straightforward bunch of one type of flower, allowing you to create an easy, affordable centrepiece.

FOOTED CONTAINERS
Urns and footed bowls are wonderful shapes for natural-style floristry. They lift up the arrangement so that the foliage and flowers have space to trail and arch – bringing movement and providing a sense of natural growth.

MULTIPLE CONTAINERS
Clusters of small containers with just a few stems each are a good way of displaying different varieties or colours of a flower. They are also an effective way of spreading colour and texture across a large surface area – such as down the centre of a long table.

LARGE-SCALE CONTAINERS

An enamel bucket is the perfect example of a large-scale container. This shape demands a bold approach, so use large-headed flowers and plenty of branching foliage to ensure the design is in proportion to the container.

TALL, NARROW CONTAINERS

The cylindrical shape of this giant jar beautifully displays tall, spire-shaped flowers. It has a narrower rim that allows the flowers to fan out, giving them space and creating a pleasing overall outline.

FAN VASES

My favourite shape of container, the fan vase has a formality that I like to contrast with wild, unruly compositions. Its wide, open shape can hold lush, abundant arrangements with plenty of variety in flowers and foliage.

Choose Your Flowers

The range of flowers in a florist or at a flower farm can be overwhelming, and you may not know where to begin. Follow these steps to ensure you achieve a good balance of shapes, textures, and colours when selecting flowers for your arrangement. When considering individual flowers, hold them up to the materials you have already selected to judge which will work together. I get a "buzz" when I find a good combination.

Look for variety and contrast in texture – such as spiky thistles next to silky petals.

*The **hornbeam** will act as the woody, **framework foliage**.*

I begin by considering shape and form before selecting colour.

1 CHOOSE YOUR PRIMARY FOCAL FLOWER

These are the flowers that will take centre stage in your design – they are normally eye-catching in colour, shape, or size, such as dahlias, sunflowers, or tulips. Also consider the container that you have chosen. Large, globe-shaped flowers work well in low, wide containers where they have plenty of elbow room, while a container with a dark, metallic finish can make bright, vibrant colours really stand out. Choosing a focal flower can be very simple – just go for one that you really like.

*This apricot-coloured waterlily **dahlia** acts as the **primary focal flower**. It is big enough and showy enough to demand centre stage in an arrangement.*

3 ADD A FINAL FLOURISH
Choose the final flourish flowers next as they will relate to your focal flowers. These wispy, more delicate flowers will often have small heads and wiry stems, adding direction and movement to the composition. Good examples are small daisy shapes, grasses, or umbel-shaped flowers. I often select these to pick up a colour in the focal flowers, creating a connection across the arrangement.

*The **zinnia** will be a **harmonizing focal flower**, matching the dahlia in colour and shape, but smaller in size.*

*Red-leaved rose acts as **decorative foliage**, providing a contrast in colour.*

*The **chocolate cosmos** will be a **final flourish**. Its deep burgundy petals pick up the colour of the freckles inside the bells of the foxglove.*

4 CHOOSE FOLIAGE
To create an abundant, lush arrangement, plenty of foliage is important. I usually aim for three different types, which allows for a good variation in texture. First select the woody **framework foliage**, which consist of longer branches, such as hornbeam or hawthorn, that will dictate the size and shape of the finished design. Then look for **filler foliage**, which is used to add volume to the arrangement. This will have shorter stems with plenty of branching side shoots, for example eucalyptus or honeysuckle. The final choice is a **decorative foliage**, which will have a contrasting shape or colour, or something to add movement to the arrangement; good examples are red-leaved rose, jasmine, and other climbers.

*The **foxglove** will be a **contrasting focal flower**. It varies in both form and colour with the dahlia.*

2 COMBINE FOCAL FLOWERS
Once you have your first focal flower, you need to select a couple of other secondary focals. These can either **harmonize** or **contrast** with your primary focal flower in shape, colour, and texture. They must not upstage your number one choice, but act in a supporting and enhancing role.

Now move on to *Create Support*

Create Support

The first step of the arrangement process is to prepare the container for the flowers. Most containers need some work behind the scenes to help anchor the stems and ensure a loose, natural-looking arrangement. For most of my arrangements, I create a cage by making a ball out of chicken wire and placing it inside the container. This provides a mesh surface for the stems to be threaded onto.

The chicken-wire support allows you to create "airy abundance" – full arrangements with space between the stems.

1 CONSTRUCT A CHICKEN-WIRE BALL

Create a chicken-wire ball that resembles a concertina, with multiple layers of wire for the stems to rest on. Don't make the ball too open, as it will struggle to support the stems, or too tight, as you may be unable to fit the stems through the gaps in the wire.

Chicken wire can be found online or in good hardware stores.

OTHER SUPPORTS

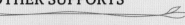

TAPE LATTICE

Chicken wire doesn't work in glass containers as it will be visible from the outside. In situations where you need to construct support for flower stems, create a lattice of clear tape over the top of the container. To do this, stick two or more parallel lines of clear tape across the container's opening, and another two or more parallel lines of tape perpendicular to the first set.

FLORAL FOAM

When a pin holder isn't big enough to support large-stemmed flowers in an arrangement, I use a small amount of floral foam in the bottom of the container to mimic a pin holder's effect. The foam is fixed in place by being pushed onto a pin holder, itself tacked to the bottom of the container. However, I use floral foam only when absolutely necessary as it can cause flowers to wilt more quickly and it is not environmentally friendly.

Floral pin holders can be used on their own or as a secondary form of support for arrangements with a chicken-wire ball. The base of the flower stems are pushed onto the pins.

2 PLACE FLORAL PIN HOLDERS

For some arrangements, chicken wire alone is not sufficient to support the flowers – particularly if you are using heavy, berried branches. For extra support, put a metal pin holder into the bottom of the container, fixing it in place using floral tack.

3 PLACE THE CHICKEN-WIRE BALL

Ensure that the ball of chicken wire is sitting flush with the rim of the container. Place a cross of tape over the top of the container to secure the ball in place. The container is filled with water at this point.

Now move on to *Position the Foliage*

Position the Foliage

The first stage of the arranging itself is the foliage. The foliage is as important as the flowers in achieving a natural floral style. It acts as the foundation of the arrangement, outlining its shape and creating a neutral and supportive background for the flowers, as well as connecting them to the container. The leaves add variety and texture, and, of course, beauty in their own right.

2 ADD THE FILLER FOLIAGE
Fill the space between the woody framework branches with shorter stems. Their purpose is to create cover and volume in the main body of the arrangement, connecting it with the container and providing a backdrop for the focal flowers.

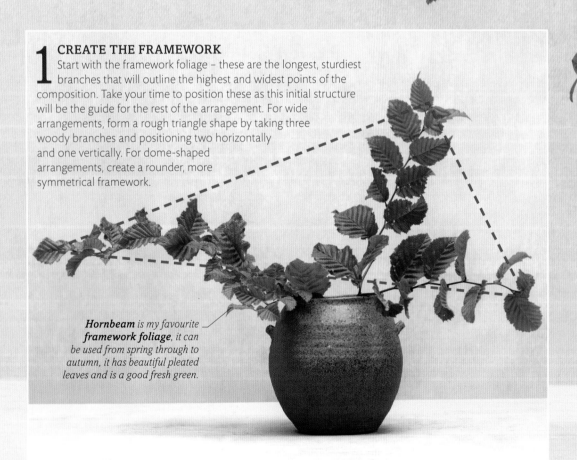

1 CREATE THE FRAMEWORK
Start with the framework foliage – these are the longest, sturdiest branches that will outline the highest and widest points of the composition. Take your time to position these as this initial structure will be the guide for the rest of the arrangement. For wide arrangements, form a rough triangle shape by taking three woody branches and positioning two horizontally and one vertically. For dome-shaped arrangements, create a rounder, more symmetrical framework.

Hornbeam is my favourite framework foliage, it can be used from spring through to autumn, it has beautiful pleated leaves and is a good fresh green.

*Eucalyptus acts as
a **filler foliage** with its
smooth, rounded leaves
and branching growth.*

3 **ADD A DECORATIVE TOUCH**
Keep the length of your decorative foliage stems fairly
long, and let them sit in the container in the direction
they would naturally grow, allowing them to arch or trail
as they would in nature. These branches will provide
a contrast colour or texture to the rest of the foliage.

***Red-leaved rose** is a **decorative foliage**.
Its plum-coloured leaves are produced on arching,
deep maroon stems. Elegant and feathery, it is
a colourful addition to your foliage palette.*

Now move on to *Place the Focal Flowers*

Place the Focal Flowers

The next step is to add the focal flowers. Think about how flowers grow on the plant – often in clusters or layers and facing in different directions. Use the plant's natural growth habit to inspire your own choices. You should also consider the arrangement's final position and the angle from which it will be viewed.

I decided to display the back of **'Totally Tangerine' dahlia** – with its intense colour and bold form it is equally as interesting from this angle.

1 PLACE THE LARGER FOCAL FLOWERS

I tend to place the leading or largest focal flowers first and then work down in size from there. For low, wide arrangements, tuck the largest focal flowers into the foliage and slightly off-centre. I have used two large dahlias in this asymmetrical arrangement but I do often work with odd numbers, which are generally easier on the eye. Prop up heavy-headed flowers by resting them on the rim of the container or foliage stems.

The daisy shape of **'Zinderella Lilac'** *zinnia with its dark centre makes it a great little focal – because it is small it can be used as an accent dotted around the larger flowers.*

Before cutting and placing a stem, hold it up to the arrangement to get a feel for where it will look most effective.

The colour of **'Warm Wishes'** *rose contains shades of all the other focal flowers – the soft peachy pinks of the 'Cafe au Lait' dahlias and zinnias, the corals and apricots of the other dahlias.*

The **'Cafe au Lait'** *dahlias are undoubtedly the main focal flowers. I cut the stems short and nestled them in low – almost resting their heavy heads on the rim of the container.*

The spire-shaped form of the **'Camelot Cream'** *foxgloves offers a striking contrast to the pillowy, round dahlias.*

2 PLACE THE CONTRASTING FOCAL FLOWERS

Position spire-shaped contrasting focal flowers along the lines of the framework foliage. The joy of working with chicken wire is that if you are not happy with where you have placed a flower you can take it out and have another go.

The soft, apricot colour of the **'Carolina Wagemans'** *dahlia harmonizes with the roses perfectly and its shape reflects that of the larger* 'Cafe au Lait' *dahlias.*

3 PLACE THE SMALLER FOCAL FLOWERS

Use the smaller focal flowers to fill in the gaps around the main players. Place them at varying angles and depths, allowing the viewer's eye to roam around the arrangement as it would if they were viewing a painting.

Now move on to *Add a Final Flourish*

Add a Final Flourish

Adding the finishing flourish is the last stage of the arrangement. These wispy, textural stems create movement and add an extra element of artistry, enhancing the leading blooms from a supporting role. I tend to select materials that are similar in colour to the focal flowers, but are a deeper or brighter shade.

I enjoy adding the final flourish the most – I find it an almost painterly experience.

The two-tone flower of **'Tinkerbell'** *tobacco plant brings together the fresh green of the hornbeam and the plum colour of the red-leaved rose.*

The maroon-coloured flowers on the wiry **great burnet** *stems make them appear to hover above the arrangement. The colour connects well with the trailing red-leaved rose.*

1 CREATE A SENSE OF MOVEMENT

Use the finishing flourish stage to create direction and movement in a design. Keep the stems long so that the flowers extend out beyond the main body of the arrangement. Curved, arched, or even kinky stems are more interesting and dynamic than straight ones.

'Creme Brulee' **phlox** *provides a creamy phlox to tie in with the foxgloves on the opposite side.*

'Peachy Keen' *mask flowers* add a peachy "pop" to enhance the colours of the focal flowers.

'Cherokee Sunset' *rudbeckia is a great colour match for the berries, as well as reflecting the form of the zinnias.*

2 ADD A "POP" OF COLOUR

Add the most colourful finishing flourish stems into areas of green across the arrangement. They will highlight or accent the arrangement, helping to connect all of the materials and unify the composition.

*I love using **viburnum berries** before they have ripened to deep red. In this arrangement they offer a textural contrast to the focal flowers, while being similar in shade.*

Conditioning & Care

To get the maximum vase life and enjoyment from your flowers, it is worth following a few simple steps to prepare the stems for arranging. Flowers have varying lengths of vase life. For example, the more fragrant a flower, the more ephemeral it will be in the vase. One general rule is to keep the vase and water as clean as possible.

Garden roses have a strong scent that shortens their vase life.

1 CUT

Before you arrange your flowers, cut the stems at a sharp angle with floral snips. This prevents the bottom of the stem sitting flush against the base of the container and increases the surface area, allowing more water to be taken up into the plant. For woody stems, use secateurs and cut about 3cm (1¼in) up the stem as well as across. Keep the blades clean and sharp so they cut well; blunt blades crush the stems and the cells that take up water.

This entire branch can be removed as part of the stripping process.

Cut stems at a sharp angle to increase water uptake.

STANDARD STEMS

Cut up the length of woody stems to maximize surface area.

Cut across the bottom of the stem for desired length.

WOODY STEMS

2 STRIP

Pull or trim all leaves, thorns, or berries that will fall below the water level in the container. If left underwater, these parts of the plant will start to decompose, bringing harmful bacteria that will shorten the vase life of the flowers.

*Keep **snapdragon** stems upright when hydrating them to ensure they remain straight.*

*This **scabious** has had all of its side shoots and foliage removed.*

***Hydrangeas** require searing before they can be arranged.*

4 HYDRATE
After being cut, flowers should be left to rest in a bucket of water overnight (conditioned) before they are arranged. This gives each stem time to take up enough water for it to be fully hydrated, meaning it will last longer in the vase. As the stems are full of water, they will also be more rigid and easier to arrange.

***Hornbeam** has thick, woody stems.*

3 SEAR
Some stems require searing after being cut to prevent them leaking sap or latex. This prolongs the flower's vase life and, as some of these secretions can be toxic, also protects other flowers in the arrangement. To sear, hold the stems 2–3cm (1in) deep in boiling water for up to 30 seconds, protecting the flowers from the steam. Then plunge into a deep bucket of water to condition.

REPLENISH

After an arrangement has been displayed for a couple of days, the water may become cloudy. This is an indication of decomposition and bacterial growth. Change the water in the container at least every 2–3 days, using fresh, warm water. This will open the cells within the stems to allow water to flow up into the flower.

Front-Facing Designs

Front-facing arrangements tend to be quite large
in scale and are normally positioned with their back against
a wall, such as on a mantelpiece or side table. This means
the back of the arrangement is not seen.

PRINCIPLES

I work at the same height from which the arrangement will be viewed. As only the front of the arrangement can be seen, there is no need to work as much material into the back. However, it will need some flowers and foliage to balance the arrangement aesthetically, but also practically – if the front is too heavy it may tip over. Fill out the back with foliage and place a few flowers, often facing away from the viewer, so that they are partially visible as you look through the arrangement. This creates a more natural, "grown-in" style, as flowers would not always naturally grow in one direction.

Fewer flowers are placed at the back of the arrangement.

SIDE VIEW

Focal flowers facing away from the front give a sense of natural growth.

These branches of framework foliage provide width and a sense of movement.

Centrepieces

A centrepiece is normally for a table that people will be sitting around for food and entertaining. It is therefore good to make it low enough to see over! It will also need to look interesting and attractive from all sides.

PRINCIPLES

I work on centrepieces sitting down with the container on a rotating wheel so that I can consider my design from all angles. Begin by selecting a low container so that the flowers will not sit too high once added. Remember to rotate the arrangement as you are working.

When the arrangement is rotated it retains its overall beauty.

ALTERNATE VIEW

From this viewpoint the roses are the focal flower within the arrangement.

How to Create a Hand-Tied Bouquet

Hand-tied bouquets are popular for weddings and as gifts. The aim is to create a full, rounded top with a narrow neck so that it is comfortable to hold. It is also a useful technique for creating an abundant arrangement for a container.

YOU WILL NEED

Focal flowers: 1 Peruvian lily stem (Alstroemeria aurea 'Friendship') • 5 roses of different varieties (Rosa 'Duchess of Cornwall', R. 'Moody Blue', R. 'Proper Job') 3 nigella stems (Nigella hispanica 'African Bride')

Foliage: 3 hornbeam branches (Carpinus betulus) • 3 Chinese forget-me-not stems (Cynoglossum amabile) • 5 apple mint stems (Mentha suaveolens)

Flowering stems: 3 astrantia stems (Astrantia major) • 2 milky bellflower stems (Campanula lactiflora) • 3 rosebay willowherb stems (Epilobium angustifolium 'Stahl Rose')

raffia or twine

1 Before starting to build your hand-tied bouquet, remove any leaves, side shoots, or thorns from the bottom half to two-thirds of the stems. Lay out all of the prepared material on a surface, grouping together flowers of the same type so that that they are easy to select.

2 Take a focal flower and hold it in your wrong hand. Add foliage and flowering stems alternately, thinking about how their colours and shapes interact. Hold the flowers in place in your palm using your thumb and forefinger. Do not use the woody hornbeam branches until step four.

3 Adjust your grip by sliding your thumb up and down your forefinger. Loosen your grip to insert new stems into the bouquet at an angle. Place each new stem beneath the existing flowers so that a dome shape to the bouquet forms. Turn the bouquet anticlockwise after every third stem to create the spiral twist to the stems.

4 Use your final stems to fill any gaps in the centre, inserting them from the top and nestling them between flowers that are already in place. Ensure that the stems are being worked in the same direction. Finish with the woodiest stems (in this case the hornbeam), which will support any softer stems, protecting them when the bouquet is tied off.

5 To tie the bouquet, loop the piece of raffia or twine around your forefinger. Then wrap it around the bouquet above your holding hand and pull the ends through the original loop. Separate the two ends, rest the bouquet on the edge of a table, and tie in a double knot.

6 Finish off the bouquet by cutting the stems so that they are uniform and neat. The bouquet should balance if placed upright on a table or work surface.

WINTER &
EARLY SPRING

Anemone

Anemone

I love anemones – their jewel-bright colours are so welcome after a long, dreary winter.

Anemones' bold colour and shape lend themselves perfectly to a simple, single-flower-type arrangement. They also have a good amount of their own green in the form of a fetching "ruff", which frames their faces. As well as their surprisingly long vase life, anemones also bring an irresistible sense of nostalgia.

STEM HEIGHT
to 80cm (32in)

FLOWER SIZE
to 8cm (3in)

LONGEVITY 7–10 days

FORM single

COLOURS blue, purple, pink, red, white

FRAGRANCE none

BEST COMPANIONS
black-leaved cow parsley, ranunculus, bluebells

FROM THE FLORIST Look for clean, tight centres without any powdery pollen. The petals should have a good, solid colour and the shape should be cupped. Check the stems for splitting and snapping.

IN THE GARDEN Anemones are cool-weather flowers, so the corms (bulbs) should be planted in the autumn to flower the following spring. They enjoy a consistently moist, well-drained soil with plenty of organic matter, and normally flower in early spring.

PREPARATION Recut the stems at a sharp angle under water and let them condition overnight with an elastic band at the top and bottom of the stems. This will set them straight before arranging.

DISPLAY As anemones open in light and heat, ensure they are given a bit of room in the vase. They work well as a single-flower-type arrangement, and can also be used as a focal flower in a mixed composition.

CARE Keep anemones in a cool room out of direct sunlight. They are thirsty flowers, so make sure you top up the vase with water every 2 days.

Anemone coronaria plants produce a succession of up to 20 single, cup-shaped blooms, each with a central eye of stamens.

Anemones represent
unfading love – in Greek mythology,
anemones grew from the spilt blood
of Adonis, lover of Aphrodite.

Nostalgic Spring Vase

I used coral-coloured anemones to create this striking arrangement, adding a little cow parsley to pick out the flowers' dark centres. The ornate, cut-glass celery vase enhances their slightly old-fashioned appearance.

YOU WILL NEED

*25 anemones
(Anemone coronaria)*

*10 black-leaved cow parsley
stems (Anthriscus sylvestris
'Ravenswing')*

floral snips

medium glass vase

ARRANGE

1 Fill the vase with water; then cut the anemone stems to around twice the height of the vase.

2 Place four or five stems in the vase to create the outline of your soft-dome-shaped arrangement.

3 Once you have a basic outline, hold the remaining stems up to the arrangment one at a time so that you can judge position and stem length. Then cut and place them appropriately. Create layers of flowers by cutting the stems to different lengths.

4 Slip the black-leaved cow parsley between the lower anemones' stems to connect the flowers to the vase.

CARE

Anemones will last 7–10 days in the vase, growing up to 5cm (2in) in that time, so trim the ends and refresh the water every 2 days.

Convallaria majalis is native to Europe, appearing in light woodland and alpine meadows. Specific varieties are also found in parts of East Asia and eastern USA.

Lily-of-the-valley

— Convallaria majalis —

Lily-of-the-valley combines a heavenly fragrance and elegant, bell-shaped, white flowers.

The form and scent of these small, delicate flowers have made them a popular wedding flower, adorning many a bridal bouquet. Their timeless beauty never seems to fall from favour, and their brief flowering period and vase life make them even more precious.

STEM HEIGHT
to 20cm (8in)

FLOWER SIZE
0.5–1cm (¼–½in)

LONGEVITY 3–5 days

FORM arching stems with small flowers

COLOURS white

FRAGRANCE
sweet and earthy

BEST COMPANIONS
peonies, ranunculus, sweet peas

FROM THE FLORIST The best stems to choose will have most of their flowers open, but a few closed buds at the top.

IN THE GARDEN Choose a shaded position to plant the "pips". You will need to be patient as they can take a few years to establish.

PREPARATION Before displaying, separate the leaves from the stems by gently pulling the two apart; this makes them easier to arrange. Recut and then place both parts in water overnight to condition.

DISPLAY The strong green foliage provides a wonderful foil for the flowers and this, along with their small stature and exquisite scent, makes them a perfect flower for arranging on their own in a small vase. Lily-of-the-valley are also a popular and traditional wedding flower, often appearing in bridal bouquets. Due to their small stature, they will need to be wired to be used in this way.

CARE Lily-of-the-valley has a short vase life because of its strong scent.

In the language of flowers, lily-of-the-valley symbolizes sweetness, humility, and a return to happiness.

Little White Bells

Small and delicate, lily-of-the-valley led me to
a simple, single-flower-type approach. I decided
to use this glass, fan-shaped posy vase as it matches
the flowers' arching stems and vintage appeal.

YOU WILL NEED

*25 lily-of-the-valley
stems and 7 leaves
(Convallaria majalis)*

floral snips

small, fan-shaped vase

ARRANGE

1 Fill the vase with water; then cut the lily-of-the-
valley stems to different lengths between two and
three times the height of the vase.

2 Position the stems in the vase so that they fan out
into a soft crescent shape. The different lengthed
stems should be irregularly spaced within the vase,
some overhanging the edges, whilst others are more
upright in the centre. You may want to trim some of
the stems further to create more variation in length.

3 Slip the leaves between the flower stems and the
vase. This will connect the flowers to the vase and
give the arrangement a natural feel.

CARE

Display the arrangement in a cool position and
refresh the water every day to prolong the vase life.
After 3–5 days the scent will fade and the flowers
will turn brown.

Freesias are a symbol of friendship. Christian Echlon named them after his friend and fellow botanist Friedrich Freese.

Freesia

Freesia

Freesias' dainty blooms adorn the top of their elegant, narrow stems in arching clusters.

Native to South Africa, freesias have a gorgeous, fruity fragrance. Their upward-facing trumpets come in a range of bright colours, each colour producing a slightly different scent. Pair freesias with rounder spring flowers as their elegant, feathery outline works well with more blousy globe shapes.

Freesia lactea is a strongly scented species. This variety is called 'Double White'.

STEM HEIGHT
10–50cm (4–20in), depending on variety; *F. lactea*, 20–40cm (8–16in)

FLOWER SIZE
2.5–6cm (1–2½in)

LONGEVITY 5–7 days

FORMS single, double

COLOURS white, yellow, orange, red, blue, green

FRAGRANCE
sweet and fruity

BEST COMPANIONS
anemones, tulips, ranunculus

FROM THE FLORIST Choose stems that are still in bud, but with the flower just beginning to open.

IN THE GARDEN Use prepared bulbs that have been heat-treated to break their dormancy, planting them in pots during autumn and keeping them in a greenhouse over winter; they will then flower in spring. They need full sun and well-drained soil. Once they begin to flower, feed them with high-potash fertilizer and use canes to support their long, thin stems.

PREPARATION Strip any of the blade-like leaves that would be under water and then cut across the bottom of the stems at a sharp angle.

DISPLAY These highly fragrant and delicate blooms are beautiful arranged on their own in a tall, fan-shaped vase that complements their natural shape.

CARE Use flower food to extend their vase life and enhance their gorgeous scent. Refresh the water every 3 days.

Fritillaries are associated with sorrow because of their drooping heads.

F. meleagris, or snake's head fritillary, thrives in areas of uncultivated land. Once found across Europe, it is now endangered in many of the areas it was once common.

Fritillary

Fritillaria

Snake's head fritillaries' unique, checkerboard pattern will add a touch of class to any arrangement.

There are many species of fritillary used for cutting. Some of my favourites are the statuesque and dramatic Persian lily (*F. persica*) and crown imperial fritillary (*F. imperialis*), as well as the delicate and wild snake's head fritillary (*F. meleagris*). Because of this range in shape and colour, fritillaries can be used both as a focal flower and finishing flourish.

STEM HEIGHT
30–150cm (1–5ft), depending on variety; *F. meleagris*, 30cm (1ft)

FLOWER SIZE
2–6cm (¾–2½in), depending on variety; *F. meleagris*, 4.5cm (1¾in)

LONGEVITY
to 2 weeks

FORMS multiple, such as snake's head, Persian lily, crown imperial

COLOURS orange, yellow, red, purple, brownish purple, depending on variety; *F. meleagris*, pink to white with purple-pink patterning

FRAGRANCE foxy

BEST COMPANIONS ranunculus, tulips, hellebores

FROM THE FLORIST Choose snake's head fritillary stems with flowers that are just starting to open, and that have a clear checkerboard pattern on their petals.

IN THE GARDEN Plant the bulbs in pots during autumn, then bring them into a greenhouse in early spring. This will force the plants to flower earlier and with an increased stem length. Once you have harvested the flowers, put them back outside and keep them watered through the summer months.

CONDITIONING Before arranging, cut the stems at a 45-degree angle and condition overnight in water. If using Persian lilies, ensure they are standing upright in the bucket so that the stems remain straight while they are conditioning.

DISPLAY Use fritillaries' nodding, bell-shaped flowers as a beautiful, naturalistic accent in a small to medium-sized mixed composition.

CARE Refresh the water every 2 days so that the flowers don't develop an unpleasant odour. This propensity to produce odour may mean it is best to place the arrangement in a well-ventilated position.

Gothic Centrepiece

The slate-coloured spires of the Persian lily fritillaries have a dramatic aesthetic that is intensified by the red shades of the ranunculus and tulips. The addition of the snake's head fritillaries provides the arrangement's final flourish.

YOU WILL NEED

10 Persian lily fritillary stems (Fritillaria persica)

3 honeywort stems (Cerinthe major)

2 honeysuckle stems (Lonicera periclymenum 'Serotina')

3 eucalyptus stems (Eucalyptus gunnii)

5 parrot tulips (Tulipa x gesneriana Parrot Group)

8 ranunculus (Ranunculus 'Pauline Chocolate')

4 black-leaf cow parsley stems (Anthriscus sylvestris 'Ravenswing')

3 heuchera leaves (Heuchera 'Pewter Moon')

10 snake's head fritillary stems (Fritillaria meleagris)

chicken wire

dark urn or urn-shaped vase

secateurs

floral snips

ARRANGE

1 Roll up some chicken wire into a ball and push it into the container. Then fill the container with water.

2 Cut the Persian lily stems to around two-and-a-half to three times the height of the container; then place them into the urn to create the outline of the arrangement. They should be relatively spaced out so that the other flowers can be added between them.

3 Cut the honeywort, honeysuckle, and eucalyptus stems to around twice the height of the container. Use their matt, green foliage to fill the space between the Persian lily stems.

4 Intersperse the strong colours of the tulips and ranunculus around the Persian lily spires. Hold them up to the arrangement to judge position and stem length; then cut and slip them into place.

5 Push in the black-leaf cow parsley stems and heuchera leaves beneath the other foliage.

6 Slip the snake's head fritillary stems into different areas of the arrangement as a final flourish. This will lift the overall appearance by creating highlights.

CARE

Recut the stems and refresh the water every 2 days. Spring bulbs (including fritillaries, ranunculus, and tulips) have a long vase life of up to 2 weeks.

Hellebore

— *Helleborus* —

Hellebores have an understated air that suits the soft light of late winter and early spring.

The flowers of the Lenten rose (*Helleborus orientalis*) are the first cut flowers of the season, and one of the longest lasting in the garden. Even after fertilization, the petals do not fall, but remain to protect the ripening seedhead. Selective breeding has produced a range of colours; some flowers have spotted centres, and others have petals with contrasting edges.

STEM HEIGHT
to 45cm (18in)

FLOWER SIZE
to 8cm (3in)

LONGEVITY 3 days if cut before seed capsules form; 2 weeks if after

FORMS single, double

COLOURS green, pink, purple, cream, white

FRAGRANCE none

BEST COMPANIONS amelanchier, anemones, snake's head fritillaries, tulips

FROM THE FLORIST Pick or choose stems that have some flowers showing seed pods – these are ripe and will last much longer in the vase.

IN THE GARDEN Hellebores enjoy moist, fertile soil and semi-shade. In these conditions they are easy to grow and will slowly bulk up and produce more flowering stems each year. New hybrids are produced every year by plant breeders, and can even occur in your own garden when varieties are cross-pollinated by insects.

PREPARATION Sear the cut stems (see pp.22–23) in hot water and score up to the neck with a sharp knife. Once seared and scored, leave them up to their necks in cool water overnight before arranging.

DISPLAY Hellebores are great minglers; their muted colours and nodding habit provide a wild, garden-grown feel to more formal spring flowers like tulips. They work well in low arrangements, which make the most of their arching stems and elegant, bowing heads.

CARE Replace the water every 3 days. If the stems are looking floppy, cut and sear them again. If they do not recover, cut off the heads and float them in a bowl to enjoy their exquisite centres.

Helleborus x hybridus cultivars are bred by pairing H. orientalis with another species. This cultivar is 'Harvington's White Speckled'.

Display hellebore arrangements
on a mantlepiece or high shelf
so you can see the flowers'
hidden centres.

Tumbling Hellebores

Here, bruise-coloured, plum, and slate
shades of hellebore create a richly coloured,
yet sombre composition, mirrored by the black
fan vase and coppery amelanchier.

YOU WILL NEED

5 amelanchier branches
(Amelanchier canadensis)

3 pieris stems
(Pieris japonica)

5 pear blossom branches
(Pyrus communis)

8 single hellebore stems
(Helleborus orientalis
'Harvington Hybrids')

4 double hellebore stems
(Helleborus 'Harvington
Double Pink')

3 anemones
(Anemone coronaria)

7 snake's head fritillary
stems (Fritillaria meleagris)

5 tulips (Tulipa 'La
Belle Epoque')

medium-sized fan vase

chicken wire

secateurs

floral snips

ARRANGE

1 Make a ball of chicken wire a little taller than the
vase and push it in so that it sits slightly above the rim.
Tape the chicken wire in place with pot tape, and then
fill the vase with water.

2 Create the outline of the low, wide arrangement
with the woody, branching amelanchier and pieris,
and three of the pear blossom stems.

3 Keeping the stems long, work in the single and
double hellebore stems between the lines of your
woody framework. Ensure that some of these are
horizontal to show off their nodding habit.

4 Highlight any darker areas with white anemones
and the remaining pear blossom. Hold them up to
the arrangement to judge position and stem length,
before cutting and placing them appropriately.

5 Add the snake's head fritillary stems and tulips
as a final flourish. Keep the meandering stems long
so they extend out of the arrangement.

CARE

Keep the arrangement in a cool position and replace
the water every 3 days. If the hellebores start to look
floppy, trim the ends and re-sear them (see pp.22–23).

Amelanchier

Single hellebore

Tulip

Double hellebore

The twisting stems of the
tulips and fritillaries provide
a sense of movement.

Anemone

Snake's head fritillary

Pear blossom

Pieris

Magnolia
Magnolia

Magnolia is one of the grandest ornamental trees, renowned for its striking form and flowers.

Magnolia's large, goblet-shaped flowers are various shades of pink, purple, and white, emerging on bare branches in early spring to create a dramatic effect. Their beautiful velvety buds, waxen flowers, and sometimes lichen-encrusted branches are best enjoyed on their own in a simple, single-flower-type arrangement.

BRANCH LENGTH
cut branches to 30–40cm (12–16in)

FLOWER SIZE
8–30cm (3–12in)

LONGEVITY 5–7 days

FORMS saucer, cup, cup and saucer, goblet, star-shaped

COLOURS white, yellow, pink, purple, green

FRAGRANCE evergreen varieties have a strong, creamy, citrus scent

BEST COMPANIONS amelanchier, tulips, ranunculus

FROM THE FLORIST Choose magnolia branches that are in bud and showing good size and colour.

IN THE GARDEN Magnolias are slow-growing shrubs that prefer a neutral to acid soil. They need sun or part shade, and shelter from strong winds.

CONDITIONING Before arranging, cut branches down to 30–40cm (12–16in) so are manageable to work with. Cut 2.5cm (1in) up the length of each stem with secateurs – this will increase the surface area so the branches can take up more water.

DISPLAY Magnolia works well in wide, asymmetrically shaped arrangements in which the branches sit horizontally. The flowers open before the leaves appear, giving the branches a strong, graphic-like outline.

CARE If picked in bud, the vase life can be up to 7 days; otherwise the petals will drop earlier. Top up the vase with fresh water every 2 days.

Magnolia x soulangeana is one of the most popular varieties, chosen for its beauty and easy cultivation.

In the language of flowers, magnolias are associated with nobility.

Magnolia Tree

This graphic arrangement focuses on the structure of magnolia's branches. Placing them horizontally in a rustic, hand-thrown pot gives them an earthiness reminiscent of the tree.

YOU WILL NEED

5 magnolia branches (Magnolia x soulangeana)

moss

round pot with rustic glazing

chicken wire

pot tape

secateurs

ARRANGE

1 Create a ball of chicken wire and push it into the pot, securing the top with a cross of tape. Then fill the pot with water.

2 Cut the branches to around 30–40cm (12–16in). Feed them into the chicken wire so they are near-horizontal – as they would be on a tree – and then tape them in place. They should be well spaced around the edge of the pot.

3 Cover the top of the pot with moss so that neither the chicken wire nor the inside of the pot is visible.

CARE

If picked in bud, the magnolia will open unblemished in the vase and last for 7 days. Replenish the water every 2 days.

Using branches with flowers at different stages of bloom adds variation to this single-flower arrangement.

Muscari are among the earliest flowers to bloom at the beginning of spring.

Muscari aucheri *are native to Turkey, and have distinctive, bright blue flowers. This variety is called* 'Blue Magic'.

Muscari

— Muscari —

An easy plant to grow, muscari has perfectly formed, conical-shaped clusters of flowers.

Muscari's common name, grape hyacinth, refers to the flowers being similar in appearance to a bunch of grapes. The blooms come in shades of blue, white, and sometimes pink, but few varieties have the stem length necessary for use as a cut flower. The best way to display them is to leave the bulbs intact and plant them up in small containers.

STEM HEIGHT
10–15cm (4–6in)

FLOWER HEAD SIZE
1–4cm (½–1½in)

LONGEVITY 2 weeks if planted intact; 7 days if cut

FORM raceme of spherical flowers

COLOURS white, blue, pink

FRAGRANCE
faint and musky

BEST COMPANIONS
narcissi, tulips, violets

FROM THE FLORIST Flowering muscari can be bought planted in pots. Ensure the stems are firm, and that only the bottom third of the flowers are open.

IN THE GARDEN Plant the small bulbs three times their height deep in the soil. This should be done in autumn, and in a position that gets full sun. They will flower in the garden during early spring, or earlier if planted in pots and brought into a greenhouse or sunny indoor windowsill.

CONDITIONING If picking from the garden, pull or pluck the stems rather than cutting them, as this will give you a little more stem length. Bunch and trim the ends, and condition in water overnight with rubber bands at the top and bottom of the stems. This will ensure the stems remain straight.

DISPLAY Their small stature means they are best arranged on their own. Keep them on the bulb so that they last longer. Alternatively, arrange them with other delicate spring flowers.

CARE They are thirsty flowers, so ensure the water is topped up every 2–3 days. If they are still on the bulb, remove the spent blooms to encourage a second flower to emerge.

Fairy-Tale Miniatures

The sky-blue clusters of muscari are small in stature, so I decided to leave the bulbs intact and plant them up in this junk shop find – a copper, footed vessel perfectly matched in proportion, colour, and texture.

YOU WILL NEED

10 sprouted muscari bulbs (Muscari aucheri 'Blue Magic')

moss

shallow vase or bowl

compost

ARRANGE

1 Place the muscari in a relatively shallow vase, keeping them quite tightly grouped in the centre, but with gaps around the edges of the vase.

2 Fill the surrounding area with compost to secure the plants in place.

3 Cover the visible compost with moss to create a turf-like effect.

CARE

This arrangement will last 2 weeks from bud stage, and the bulbs can then be planted outdoors. Water every 2–3 days.

Narcissus

Narcissus

With their cheery colours and gorgeous scent, narcissi are one of the most popular cut flowers.

Narcissi make up for their limited choice in colour with an amazing variety of forms. These range from the well-known trumpet form of the daffodil, to the more unusual split corona – which looks more like an exotic orchid. Lending themselves to informal arrangements, narcissi look lovely when a few varieties are combined in a simple jug or vase.

In the language of flowers, narcissi symbolize egotism. However, they are more generally associated with the arrival of spring.

STEM HEIGHT
30–40cm (12–16in), depending on variety; *N.* 'Geranium', 35cm (14in)

FLOWER SIZE 5–10cm (2–4in), depending on variety; *N.* 'Geranium', to 6cm (2½in)

LONGEVITY 7–10 days

FORMS multiple, such as trumpet, double, triandrus, jonquilla, tazetta, poeticus, bulbocodium, split corona

COLOURS yellow, cream, orange, peach

FRAGRANCE strong and sweet

BEST COMPANIONS anemones, muscari, tulips

FROM THE FLORIST Choose narcissi that are in bud, as these will open even when cut. The buds should be a good size and colour.

IN THE GARDEN Plant the bulbs three times their height deep in the soil during early autumn. They can be planted either in a flower border or in grass. When picking narcissi, pinch the stems rather than cut them. Leave all the foliage to die back and then feed the bulb so it will bloom again the following year.

PREPARATION Cut the stems at an angle and leave to condition overnight in water.

DISPLAY Narcissi exude a latex serum that is poisonous to other flowers. Arrange them on their own to extend the vase life of any arrangement they are in. However, narcissi do combine well in a bouquet with other spring bulbs, such as tulips, anemones, and muscari – just ensure the stems are well rinsed to minimize damage to the other flowers.

CARE Refresh the water every 2 days, recutting the stems each time.

Narcissus '**Geranium**' *is a tazetta-type narcissus, bearing three or four flowers on each stem.*

Narcissus Cloud

I prefer to display narcissi on their own because they reduce the vase life of other flowers. They are great to throw together in a loose arrangement – this arrangement is a hand-tied bouquet held together by the rim of a mug.

YOU WILL NEED

30 narcissus stems (Narcissus 'Geranium'), or enough for the stems to fill the neck of your tankard

medium-sized tankard

floral snips

ARRANGE

1 Pour water into the tankard. Then arrange the stems in your hand as you would a hand-tied bouquet (see pp.26–27), ensuring that there is a variation in height. Stop at the point you would tie the bouquet.

2 Hold the bunch up to the tankard to judge where to cut before carefully trimming the stems so that they create a flat base.

3 Place the narcissi into the tankard, retaining the slight twisting position of the stems.

CARE

Cut the stems every 2 days, refreshing the water each time. The arrangement should last for 7–10 days.

Narcissus 'Geranium' is a favourite variety of mine as it has a great scent and a good stem length.

The Latin name, *Pieris*, is derived from Pieria – the home of the Muses in Greek mythology.

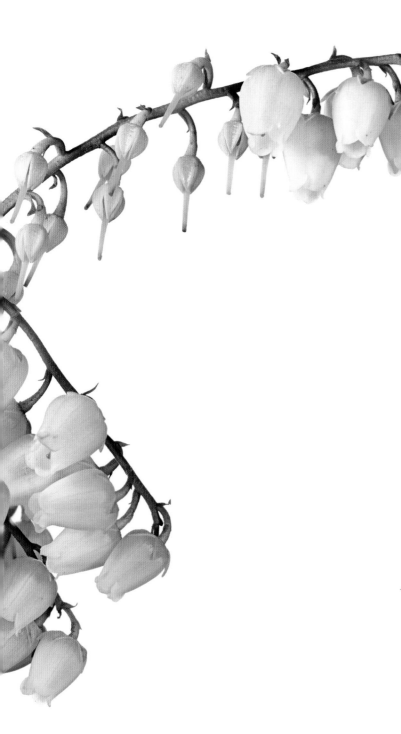

Pieris

Pieris japonica

The beautiful draping flowers of pieris add valuable texture and movement to spring arrangements.

Pieris' cascading sprays of tiny, waxy, urn-shaped, white bells give the impression of hundreds of lily-of-the-valley backed by rosettes of glossy evergreen foliage. This combination of foliage and flowers makes it a useful filler, particularly draped over the edge of a vase. With its short flowering season, pieris is normally only available for 2–3 weeks of the year.

BRANCH LENGTH cut branches to desired length

FLOWER SIZE 5–8mm (¼–⅜in)

LONGEVITY 7 days

FORM stems of hanging, urn-shaped flowers

COLOURS white, red, pink

FRAGRANCE honey

BEST COMPANIONS anemones, cherry or pear blossom, hellebores

FROM THE FLORIST Check that the florets are not shedding by giving the branch a shake. The leaves should be glossy and in good condition.

IN THE GARDEN Plant pieris in full sun or partial shade, in an area that is sheltered from wind; the soil should be neutral to acid. Harvest the flowers in late winter or early spring.

CONDITIONING Cut 2.5cm (1in) up the woody stem as this increases the surface area for the plant to take in water. Then sit in deep water overnight to rehydrate them. Ensure that none of the flowers or leaves fall below the waterline.

DISPLAY Pieris' arching, cascading habit works well as a collar in hand-tied bouquets, creating a trailing effect. This effect can also be created by letting it fall over the edge of a vase in a mixed composition. Smaller pieces can be used to great effect in buttonholes and floral circlets.

CARE Refresh the water every 2 days to stop the florets from dropping quickly.

Pieris japonica is poisonous to animals and humans and so should not be ingested.

In Chinese culture, cherry blossom is associated with feminine beauty.

Cherry Blossom

— Prunus —

Brief and beautiful, the eruption of cherry blossom's frothy petals heralds spring like nothing else.

The Japanese name for cherry blossom is *sakura*. In Japan, cherry blossom is revered, symbolizing the transience of life. This is due to the all-too-fleeting nature of its breath-taking beauty – it is not long before the pink and white petals fall to the ground like confetti.

BRANCH LENGTH
cut branches to
desired length

FLOWER SIZE
to 2cm (¾in)

LONGEVITY 7 days

FORMS single, double

COLOURS white, pink

FRAGRANCE none

BEST COMPANIONS
anemones, tulips,
ranunculus

FROM THE FLORIST Buy cherry blossom branches when they in bud, but ensure they are of a good size and showing good colour.

IN THE GARDEN Cherry blossom is grown as an ornamental tree, so it may be some years before you are able to cut branches. Foraging in a mindful way may be an easier option.

CONDITIONING Cut 2.5cm (1in) up the length of each stem with secateurs – this will increase the surface area so that the branches can take up more water. It is possible to force the branches, so they can be enjoyed a bit earlier in the year. To do this, bring them into a warm environment with low light conditions and place in tepid water.

DISPLAY In mixed arrangements, cherry blossom branches can provide structure for accompanying flowers to be worked around. They also make striking and dramatic arrangements on their own. You will need a sturdy container to support their weight.

CARE Refresh the water every 2 days, especially if you are using a glass vessel, as woody branches turn water murky very quickly.

Prunus x yedoensis is a hybrid of Prunus speciosa and Prunus pendula f. ascendens. It appears naturally in Japan, but is also widely cultivated around the world.

Cherry Tree Jug

To create a striking statement piece, I have arranged cherry blossom on its own – the stark, knobbly branches contrasting beautifully with the soft, marshmallow-like flowers. I selected these pieces for their arching lines.

YOU WILL NEED

6 cherry blossom branches (Prunus x yedoensis)

large jug

chicken wire

secateurs

pot tape

ARRANGE

1 Place a ball of chicken wire in the top of the jug and tape it in place. Then fill the jug with water.

2 Cut the cherry blossom branches to around two to three times the height of the jug. Position them so that the areas of flowers give the arrangement a denser core. Tape the branches to the chicken wire to secure them in place.

3 If necessary, prune some of the branches so that the arrangement isn't too dense. The arching lines of the bare branches should be visible as they extend out of the main body of the arrangement.

CARE

Refresh the water every 2 days and the arrangement will last for around 7 days.

Ranunculus

Ranunculus

Composed of layer upon layer of tissue-like petals, ranunculus are one of my favourite flowers.

Ranunculus come in an impressive array of shades that vary from vividly bright to soft and muted, so can be used to create a range of moods and aesthetics. As the hollow stems can sometimes struggle to support the heavy heads, place these flowers on the lip of the container or surround them with other blooms so that they are well supported.

STEM HEIGHT
20–45cm (8–18in)

FLOWER SIZE
3–5cm (1¼–2in)

LONGEVITY 7–10 days

FORMS single, double

COLOURS red, yellow, orange, pink, white

FRAGRANCE none

BEST COMPANIONS
anemones, tulips, sweet peas, Icelandic poppies

FROM THE FLORIST Choose flowers with strong stems as the necks can be prone to breaking. The petals should be in a firm, cupped shape.

IN THE GARDEN Plant the soaked claws (bulbs) in the autumn in moist, well-drained soil that has been prepared with plenty of organic matter. Mulch well if growing outdoors. Once they start flowering in the spring, keep picking and feeding them to encourage continual flowering for 4–6 weeks.

CONDITIONING Remove the leaves from the stems before arranging. As the stems are hollow, they need to be recut under water to ensure any air trapped within them is released.

DISPLAY As they have relatively heavy heads compared to their thin necks, it is generally better to cut the stems of the larger-headed flowers short. This allows them to rest their chins on the rim of the vase, or on other flowers and foliage. Use smaller heads as a finishing flourish, floating above the rest of the arrangement on their narrow, often-kinky stems.

CARE They are thirsty flowers, so keep an eye on the water level. As ranunculus will not tolerate debris in the vase, refresh the water every 2 days.

Ranunculus 'Pauline Chocolate' *has a "double" form – this means it has more petals than a variety with a "single" form.*

In the language of flowers,
ranunculus symbolize
radiant charm.

Picotee Petals

I particularly love picotee ranunculus' painterly petals with their contrasting edges. To really show them off, I chose a wide bowl shape, allowing plenty of space around each flower. The raised bowl is an invitation for a wide, asymmetrically shaped arrangement – perfect for a centrepiece.

YOU WILL NEED

3 amelanchier branches (Amelanchier canadensis)

3 spiraea stems (Spiraea x arguta)

7 ranunculus in a variety of pastel colours (Ranunculus asiaticus)

2 Icelandic poppies (Papaver nudicaule)

3–5 parrot tulips (Tulipa 'Apricot Parrot')

3 heuchera leaves (Heuchera 'Pewter Moon')

3 snake's head fritillary stems (Fritillaria meleagris)

ceramic, footed bowl

chicken wire

pot tape

secateurs

floral snips

ARRANGE

1 Tape a ball of chicken wire into the container. Then pour in water.

2 Cut the three woody, structural branches of the amelanchier to about three times the height of the container. Use these to create the triangular outline of your arrangement.

3 Place the spiraea between the amelanchier stems, allowing some of it to trail downwards.

4 Hold the ranunculus, poppies, and tulips up to the arrangement one at a time in order to judge the required position and stem length. Then cut and place them into the arrangement appropriately.

5 Slip a few heuchera leaves between the foliage and container. Finally, dot the snake's head fritillary stems in the gaps of the arrangement for a finishing flourish.

CARE

Refresh the water every 2 days as the ranunculus cannot tolerate bacterial build up. The arrangement will last for up to 7 days.

Pussy Willow

Salix

At the start of the year, pussy willow is one of the first things I venture into the garden to pick.

Pussy willow is known for its soft, silvery grey catkins that appear on long, dark, slender stems. One of the earliest signs of spring, these catkins provide an important early source of pollen and nectar for bees and other insects. The tactile nature of the branches contrasts beautifully with other early spring flowers in both form and colour.

BRANCH LENGTH
cut branches to
desired length

FLOWER SIZE
4cm (1½in)

LONGEVITY 7–10 days
in water; longer if dried

FORMS catkin

COLOURS silvery white

FRAGRANCE none

BEST COMPANIONS
anemones, hellebores,
narcissi

FROM THE FLORIST Select catkins (the downy flowers) that are still a good silvery grey with an almost metallic sheen. They should have not started to bloom – this is when they are showing a good deal of yellow pollen.

IN THE GARDEN Willows prefer a moist, well-drained soil. Catkins are produced on the previous year's growth, so prune willows before midsummer so that stems have time to regrow and produce catkins for the following year.

CONDITIONING Chop the branches down to the desired length before arranging, cutting at a sharp angle and placing them in water afterwards.

DISPLAY The tall, straight stems of pussy willow work well in large, narrow containers either on their own, or mixed with other early-spring-flowering branches and bulbs.

CARE Pussy willow can be dried in the vase to prevent it flowering. To do this, remove the water and keep it in a cool position.

In Polish folklore, a willow tree pulled a group of drowning kittens out of a river. The furry blooms appear where the kittens held on to the branches.

Salix caprea is found across Europe, as well as Western and Central Asia. A separate species – S. discolor – is native to North America.

Lilac

Syringa vulgaris

This garden favourite has billowy panicles of richly fragrant flowers.

Lilacs bridge the gap between spring and summer. While the flowers are commonly found in a range of lilac and purple shades, pink and white varieties are also available. With their old-fashioned charm, lilacs lend a vintage feel to arrangements, working particularly well when combined with other spring foliage and flowering branches.

STEM HEIGHT
cut branches to
desired length

FLOWER SIZE
5–8mm (¼–⅜in)

LONGEVITY 5 days

FORMS single, double

COLOURS purple,
pink, white

FRAGRANCE
sweet and heady

BEST COMPANIONS
blossom, guelder roses,
ranunculus

FROM THE FLORIST Select branches where most of the flower panicles are open, as tight buds will not develop after being cut.

IN THE GARDEN As slow-growing, hardy shrubs, lilacs should be pruned immediately after flowering. This will ensure that more flowering branches appear the following year.

PREPARATION Remove the majority of the leaves. Cut 2.5cm (1in) up the stems with secateurs after cutting across at an angle – this creates more surface area for the plant to take up water. Before arranging, condition them overnight in warm water up to their necks.

DISPLAY Lilacs make beautiful, frothy, scented filler flowers in mixed spring arrangements. Their soft colours work well with other blossoming branches and spring bulbs.

CARE Change the water every 2 days, adding floral preservative. Arrange them on their own to preserve their vase life as hormones released from other plants will cause them to wilt more quickly.

In the language of flowers, lilacs represent new-found love. White lilacs are said to represent innocence.

Syringa vulgaris originates from Eastern Europe, but is now naturalized throughout Europe and in parts of North America.

Tulip

Tulipa

A top favourite for many, the tulip celebrates spring with a real panache.

I always feel spoilt by the overwhelming choice of colour and variety this flamboyant flower provides after the limited palette of the winter months. Unlike most other flowers, tulips continue to grow after they are cut, stretching and bending towards the light. This makes them an unpredictable, but fascinating addition to an arrangement.

STEM HEIGHT
15–75cm (6–30in), depending on variety; viridiflora group, 40–55cm (16–22in)

FLOWER SIZE
6–10cm (2½–4in), depending on variety; viridiflora group, 8cm (3in)

LONGEVITY 7–10 days

FORMS multiple, such as single, double, lily-flowered, fringed, viridiflora, parrot, and others

COLOURS white, red, orange, yellow, green, purple, pink, brown, apricot, black

FRAGRANCE some varieties have a subtle, freesia-like scent

BEST COMPANIONS anemones, cherry or pear blossom, ranunculus

FROM THE FLORIST Choose stems with closed flowers showing a good flush of colour. The flowers should be held on upright stems and the leaves squeaky and firm to the touch.

IN THE GARDEN Grow tulips as an annual, planting the bulbs 10cm (4in) deep and 10cm (4in) apart in late autumn or early winter when the ground is cold. In spring, pull the stems (bulb and all) out of the ground to harvest.

PREPARATION Cut off the bulb and the white at the bottom of the stem. Then peel off all of the leaves except the top two (this prevents the plant becoming saturated) and condition in water overnight.

DISPLAY Definitely a focal flower, tulips look wonderful both on their own and with cherry or pear blossom. When arranging, leave plenty of space around the flowers because they grow in the vase. A footed container will lift up the plants, allowing the stems to dangle so that you can make the most of their ever-changing stems.

CARE Tulips may need reorganizing and retrimming every couple of days as they grow. Top up the water level every 2 days.

Tulipa **'Spring Green'** *is a viridiflora group cultivar that develops a green stripe on its white petals when fully mature.*

In 1630s Amsterdam, single tulip bulbs were thought to have been sold for as much as ten times a skilled craftsman's annual salary.

Spring Show-Stopper

This bold statement piece would look great in a large entrance foyer or as a centrepiece in a lofty space. To minimize the weight I have used a faux urn and a plastic bowl filled with chicken wire that sits perfectly in the top.

YOU WILL NEED

5 hawthorn branches
(Crataegus monogyna)

7 plum blossom branches
(Prunus mume)

4 eucalyptus branches
(Eucalpytus gunnii)

6 pieris stems
(Pieris japonica)

8 lily-flowered tulips (Tulipa
'White Triumphator')

6 peony tulips (Tulipa
'Mount Tacoma')

4 anemones (Anemone
coronaria 'The Bride')

10 viridiflora tulips (Tulipa
'Spring Green')

5 Solomon's seal stems
(Polygonatum x hybridum)

2 crown imperial fritillary
stems (Fritillaria imperialis)

large urn

plastic bowl – to fit snugly
into the top of the urn

chicken wire

pot tape

secateurs

ARRANGE

1 Make a chicken-wire ball and tape it into the bowl. Then fill the bowl with water and place it in the urn.

2 Cut the woody hawthorn and plum blossom branches to at least twice the height of the urn. Position them in the chicken wire to create an asymmetrical shape, then tape them in place.

3 Use the eucalyptus to fill the central area above the urn with green. Slip the pieris stems under the foliage so it hangs over the edge of the urn.

4 Place the tulips and anemones between the lines of the hawthorn and plum blossom branches. Cut some of their stems shorter to create layers of flowers. Don't be afraid to position them in clusters rather than dotting them equally throughout the arrangement.

5 Add the Solomon's seal, ensuring the arching stems and hanging flowers can be clearly seen.

6 Add the pair of show-stopping fritillary to the right side of the arrangement. Ensure the stems are long enough to extend out past the other flowers.

CARE

The tulips will grow in the vase, so retrim and reposition them every 2 days to maintain the arrangement's balance and proportion. Replenish the water every 2 days and the arrangement should last for a week.

LATE SPRING & EARLY SUMMER

Alchemists once believed that raindrops harvested from lady's mantle leaves could turn metal into gold.

Lady's Mantle

Alchemilla mollis

These frothy, green flowers with their downy foliage are perfect for a country-style arrangement.

A mainstay of early summer floristry, lady's mantle works equally well with bright or muted colour palettes, and its soft, fluffy form will adapt to any kind of arrangement. It can be grown in two ways: planted in the shade it will hold its strong, green colour, but planted in a sunny position it will grow taller and the flowers will turn yellow.

Alchemilla mollis is a hardy plant that will grow in a variety of soils and conditions.

STEM HEIGHT to 60cm (24in)

FLOWER SIZE 2–3mm ($\frac{1}{16}$–$\frac{1}{8}$in)

LONGEVITY 10–14 days

FORM clusters of tiny flowers

COLOURS green, yellow

FRAGRANCE none

BEST COMPANIONS roses, sweet peas, cornflowers

FROM THE FLORIST Ensure the flowers are frothy and not too tight. Do not choose flowers that look dry.

IN THE GARDEN Lady's mantle spreads rapidly, so lift and divide it every 3 years. Once the flowers turn yellow, prune the whole plant and water well for a second flush of leaves and sometimes flowers in autumn; this will also reduce spreading.

CONDITIONING Be sure to cut the stems at an angle and condition in water overnight to prolong the plant's vase life.

DISPLAY The flowers are a great filler, and create a wonderful backdrop for other blooms. Cut the stems short and work them into floristry foam to create garlands and floral balls. Alternatively, keep the stems long and use them in hand-tied bouquets and front-facing or centrepiece arrangements. Use the leaves to create a collar of foliage when arranging in vases.

CARE Refresh the water every 2 days to maximize the vase life.

Allium

—— Allium ——

With globe-shaped flowers on long straight stems, alliums create a bold statement.

Alliums are an exclamation mark in the garden and in the vase, but take some thought to arrange effectively. Each allium globe is made up of lots of small, star-shaped flowers that, as alliums are part of the onion family, have a slightly oniony scent. As they age, some of the flowers turn into green seed heads, and their scent intensifies.

STEM HEIGHT
to 1m (3ft)

FLOWER HEAD SIZE
5–10cm (2–4in)

LONGEVITY
to 2 weeks

FORMS globe-shaped flower head, cluster of pendant (hanging) flowers

COLOURS pink, purple, blue, white

FRAGRANCE
mild onion

BEST COMPANIONS
ammi, foxgloves, Solomon's seal, bearded irises

FROM THE FLORIST A fresh allium will have half of its star-shaped flowers open.

IN THE GARDEN Alliums are very easy to grow. They like well-drained soil and enjoy full sun. In autumn, plant the bulbs three times their length deep in the soil.

CONDITIONING A drop of bleach in the water will help to minimize the oniony smell.

DISPLAY To enjoy the detail of the flower, nestle alliums into bouquets or take advantage of their long stem length by placing them in large-scale arrangements. Their starry globes combine well with tall, spire-shaped flower heads and arching stems. Alternatively, display them alongside the softening influence of umbel shapes, such as ammi, or bold outlines, such as irises.

CARE They have a long vase life of up to 2 weeks. Be sure to change the water every 2–3 days to prevent an oniony odour developing.

Allium hollandicum **'Purple Sensation'**
is a popular variety among gardeners as it has a stable form and colour, and is relatively resistant to pests and diseases.

In the language of flowers, alliums symbolize prosperity.

Peruvian Lily

— *Alstroemeria* —

Flowering for months in the garden and weeks in the vase, Peruvian lillies deserve more recognition.

Peruvian lilies are tuberous perennials that originate from South America but, despite their common name, are not related to lilies. At the top of each stem, they produce clusters of flowers that have centres that are streaked with burgundy "brushstrokes".

STEM HEIGHT
to 1m (3ft)

FLOWER SIZE
3.5–10cm (1⅜–4in)

LONGEVITY to 3 weeks

FORM cluster of
single flowers

COLOURS purple,
peach, yellow, orange,
red, pink, white

FRAGRANCE none

BEST COMPANIONS
roses, dill, sunflowers

FROM THE FLORIST Check the smaller buds have not been removed and that there is no foliage on the stem.

IN THE GARDEN Preferring full sun and rich, well-drained soil, the fleshy roots will spread underground and can become invasive. Cover with compost in the winter – especially in the first couple of years. To encourage more flowering stems, pull rather than cut the stems when harvesting.

CONDITIONING Ensure all of the foliage has been removed from the stems. Wear gloves as the sap can irritate the skin.

DISPLAY The loose cluster of flowers nestles in beautifully amongst larger single flower heads. The individual florets often have long enough stems to be used on their own in floral garlands.

CARE Refresh the water every 2 days and all the closed buds will open, elongating the vase life.

The Peruvian lily was once known as the "Lily of the Incas".

Alstroemeria aurea 'Friendship'
is a tall variety for outdoor cultivation,
combining soft, buttery yellow with
a tinge of pink.

Ammi

— Ammi —

Ammi's branching stems and lacy flowers are great fillers, creating volume in a light, transparent way.

Looking like a refined version of cow parsley, ammi brings a meadowy character to summer arrangements. It is easy to grow, and the best lacy filler flower for this time of year – pick armfuls of stems to create large fluffy clouds in a vase. Ammi is loved by pollinating insects.

STEM HEIGHT
to 1m (3ft)

FLOWER HEAD SIZE
15–30cm (6–12in)

FORM umbel of
small flowers

LONGEVITY 10 days

COLOUR white

FRAGRANCE carroty

BEST COMPANIONS
roses, scabious,
delphiniums

FROM THE FLORIST Make sure the main flower head (known as an "umbel") is not shedding petals, but is fully open and a fresh, greenish white. Ammi does not continue to open once picked, and is more likely to droop if cut when too green.

IN THE GARDEN This hardy annual is easy to grow from seed directly or in plug trays. Grow in a sunny position sheltered from the wind. It will not re-bloom when cut, so sow the seeds monthly through spring for a steady supply of flowers. Sowing in summer will produce better growth the following spring.

CONDITIONING Cut the hollow stems under water to avoid creating an airblock. Use warm water with flower food to condition.

DISPLAY Ammi is a fantastic filler flower – its flat, horizontal umbels contrast beautifully with spire shapes, and it can be combined with button and daisy shapes to create a meadow effect. Cut it short and nestle it in amongst blousier blooms to create a frothy space between denser flowers.

CARE Repeat the process of trimming under refreshed warm water every 2 days.

Records of ammi's use as
a remedy for skin conditions
date back to Ancient Egypt.

Ammi majus '**Snowflake**' *is
a robust variety of the species
that has strong stems.*

Ammi Burst

Often classed as a filler, ammi is equally lovely arranged on its own in a big, frothy cloud. Because I have only used one type of flower, I have selected stems in different stages of maturity to create variety.

YOU WILL NEED

20 ammi stems at varying stages of bloom (Ammi majus 'Snowflake')

tall, cylindrical jug

floral snips

ARRANGE

1 Fill the container with water and cut the ammi stems to about three times the height of the container.

2 Place the stems into the container so that they form a loose, round shape. Hold the stems up to the arrangement to judge position and stem length, before trimming and placing appropriately. Be sure to intermingle the young, green flower heads with their whiter, more mature counterparts.

CARE

Top up the water level every 2 days. The flowers will begin to shed after about 5 days.

In the language of flowers, astrantias symbolize strength, courage, and protection.

Astrantia

Astrantia major

Astrantias do not immediately stand out, but a closer look reveals their delicate beauty.

Adorning arrangements with their precious tufted florets surrounded by serrated leaves, astrantias always remind me of vintage costume jewellery. Each branched stem holds at least six flower heads, each of which is comprised of multiple tiny flowers. Their intricate detail makes them the perfect filler flower.

STEM HEIGHT
30–90cm (12–36in)

FLOWER HEAD SIZE
2–3cm (¾–1¼in)

LONGEVITY to 2 weeks

FORM clusters of small flowers

COLOURS green, pink, red, white

FRAGRANCE musty

BEST COMPANIONS
roses, sweet peas, nigella

FROM THE FLORIST The central flower on the stem must be fully open, and the outer flowers well on their way to being open, otherwise the stems will droop. Check that they do not smell musty, or that the bracts (the petal-like leaves that surround the tiny, inner flowers) have no signs of discolouration, as this indicates that they have been in storage too long.

IN THE GARDEN Plant in full sun during autumn or spring, providing lots of moisture to produce plants with a good stem length. Cut back after flowering for a second flush of flowers in autumn.

CONDITIONING Cut the stems at a sharp angle and condition overnight in warm water.

DISPLAY Pair with other flowers with a vintage appeal, such as roses. Strongly scented flowers are beneficial as they will mask astrantia's slightly unpleasant odour. Astrantia holds well out of water, so use it for floral crowns and buttonholes.

CARE Refresh the water every 2 days to maximize the vase life.

Astrantia major will self-seed and produce flowers with lots of variation in size and colour.

Cornflower

Centaurea cyanus

Grown en masse, this electric blue wildflower creates a jaw-dropping effect – the bluest of blues.

Also known as "batchelor's buttons", cornflowers have small flower heads that are densely packed with ragged-looking petals on grey-green wiry stems. Blue is the best-known colour, but cornflowers also come in whites, reds, pinks, and purples. The burgundy variety 'Black Ball' is particularly good.

STEM HEIGHT
20–80cm (8–32in) depending on variety; *C. cyanus* 'Blue Ball', to 30cm (12in)

FLOWER HEAD SIZE
2.5–4cm (1–1½in)

LONGEVITY 7–10 days

FORM flower head with different coloured and shaped outer and inner florets

COLOURS blue, white, pink, purple, red

FRAGRANCE none

BEST COMPANIONS
ammi, grasses, poppies

FROM THE FLORIST The buds will not open once the stem is cut, so select stems with open, fresh, vibrantly coloured flowers. They are normally sold in bunches.

IN THE GARDEN Cornflowers are hardy annuals grown from seed each year in late summer or spring; this makes them an extremely cost-effective cut flower to grow. They will keep flowering over a few months if the spent flowers are removed promptly. If the soil is fertile the plants will get very tall, so they must be supported. They are loved by pollinating insects for their nectar, and by birds for their seed.

CONDITIONING Remove any leaves that fall below the surface of the water – these will turn slimy very quickly.

DISPLAY Cornflower is the perfect flower for a meadow-style arrangement, working well with cultivated forms of annual wildflowers. Combine cobalt blue varieties with equally strong-coloured flowers, casually arranging them in a jam jar or jug.

CARE Refresh the water every 2 days.

Cornflowers are a symbol of elegance and delicacy.

Centaurea cyanus *was once widespread, but has now become endangered in its natural environment. This variety is called* 'Blue Ball'.

Clematis

Clematis

A well-established garden favourite, clematis has now become a florist's staple.

With more than 200 varieties, clematis comes in an array of shapes and colours. Different species flower during each season, from the soft pinks of the early-flowering *C. montana* through to the autumnal and yellow *C. tangutica*. Herbaceous varieties are commonly seen in florists and make a beautiful focal flower in a bouquet.

STEM HEIGHT climbers, up to 15m (49ft); perennials or subshrubs, 0.3–6m (1–20ft); *C. x durandii*, 1–2m (3–6½ft)

FLOWER SIZE 1–20cm (½–8in), depending on variety; *C. x durandii*, 6–8cm (2½–3in)

LONGEVITY 7–10 days

FORMS multiple, such as single, double, saucer-shaped, bell-shaped, tulip-shaped

FRAGRANCE none; *C. montana* varieties smell of sweet vanilla

COLOURS blue, purple, yellow, red, pink, white, cream

BEST COMPANIONS roses, ranunculus, dahlias

FROM THE FLORIST Look for buds that are just cracking open.

IN THE GARDEN Plant in moisture-retentive, well-drained soil with its feet in the shade and its head in the sun. Most varieties are self-clinging, but provide support or a shrub for herbaceous types to climb through. Feed regularly and wait about 3 years for an abundance of flowers. All require pruning, but easiest are herbaceous varieties – just cut back in early spring.

CONDITIONING If harvesting from the garden, cut the stems long enough to retain some of the woody section – this will help them to take up water. Condition overnight in a deep bucket of water. They can then be cut to the desired length.

DISPLAY Clematis's trailing nature is wonderful in asymmetrical, loose, hand-tied bouquets. They also work well in footed vessels where they can be allowed to dangle over the edge of the vase, exposing their twisting stems and adding a sense of movement to mixed compositions.

CARE Keep the arrangement out of direct sunlight as clematis will wilt in warm conditions. Refresh the water every 2 days.

Clematis x durandii is a summer-flowering, herbaceous perennial that produces large, solitary, saucer-shaped flowers.

According to the language of flowers, clematis are associated with art and ingenuity.

Delphinium

Delphinium

Delphinium's majestic spires never fail to impress with their intense colour and bold shape.

Their tall stems are densely covered in individual florets that can be found in colours ranging from almost turquoise-blue to the deepest indigo-purples and dusky pinks. Florets can be single or double, the double forms having more petals, and their centres carry a tuft of sepals (called a "bee"), which creates an effective contrast to the outer petals.

STEM HEIGHT 0.6–2m (2–6½ft), depending on variety; *D.* Elatum Group, 1.5–2m (5–6½ft)

FLORET SIZE 2–7cm (¾–2¾in), depending on variety; *D.* Elatum Group, 6cm (2½in)

LONGEVITY 5–7 days

FORMS spike of single or double florets

COLOURS purple, blue, green, yellow, orange, red, pink, cream, white, grey

FRAGRANCE none

BEST COMPANIONS ammi, campanulas, peonies

FROM THE FLORIST Look for spires that have about three quarters of the florets open – blooms in tight bud will not open once cut. Delphiniums do not transport well so try to buy from a local grower.

IN THE GARDEN Delphiniums are demanding flowers. They enjoy full sun, fertile soil, and plenty of water, and they must be supported. After flowering, cut the entire plant right back, then water and feed well for a smaller, second flush in autumn; use these shorter spires for table centrepieces and bouquets.

CONDITIONING Strip any leaves that fall below the water line. Fill a deep bucket and cut stems at an angle under water to prevent air blocks. As the stems are hollow, cover the bottom when lifting them to prevent water spillages.

DISPLAY They are perfect for large statement pieces, such as pedestal arrangements and urns. Pair them with umbel-shaped flower heads, such as ammi and dill, whose flat forms offer a contrast in shape.

CARE Refresh the water every 2 days and the flowers should last 5–7 days before the bottom florets shatter. Delphiniums are sensitive to other plants – keep them away from fruit and other flowers to increase vase life.

The individual delphinium florets often have long enough stems to be used in buttonholes or garlands.

Delphinium '**Dusky Maidens**' *is a single-form variety that is part of the* Elatum Group – *the group most commonly grown in gardens.*

Sapphire Spires

The delphinium spires work perfectly with the green glass and narrow shape of the jar. The bupleurum breaks up the delphiniums' vertical lines, its acid-green colour acting as a highlight against the bright blue florets.

YOU WILL NEED

12 delphinium spikes
(Delphinium x elatum
New Millennium Series)

7 bupleurum stems
(Bupleurum rotundifolium)

large glass jar

floral snips

ARRANGE

1 Fill the jar with water. Then cut the delphinium stems to varying lengths between three times and twice the height of the jar.

2 Using the varying lengths of delphinium stems, create a fan shape. Position three of the shortest stems at an angle around the edge of the jar. Add in another layer of slightly longer stems, and finish with the tallest stems sitting fairly upright in the centre.

3 Cut the bupleurum stems to about twice the height of the jar – they should not be tall enough to interrupt the fan-shaped outline of the delphiniums when they are added later.

4 Finish by nestling the bupleurum into the jar between the delphinium stems.

CARE

Position the arrangement in shade away from other flowers and fruit – delphiniums are sensitive to sunlight and other plants. The arrangement should last for a week.

Dianthus barbatus *are native to southern Europe. This variety is called* 'Hollandia Purple Crown'.

Sweet William

— Dianthus barbatus —

A cottage-garden classic, sweet William is a jolly flower with its light, spicy fragrance.

Often undervalued, the sweet William, if grown well, is an invaluable flower for early summer. Its dense head is made up of lots of smaller florets, which come in white and a range of pinks, purples, and reds. The darker-coloured varieties have a distinct, clove-like scent.

STEM HEIGHT
to 70cm (28in)

FLOWER HEAD SIZE
8–12cm (3–4¾in)

LONGEVITY 7–10 days

FORM flower head of small flowers

COLOURS pink, purple, red, peach, white

FRAGRANCE clove-like

BEST COMPANIONS alchemilla, peonies, roses, stocks, sweet peas

FROM THE FLORIST Check the open florets look fresh, and that there are more moss-like buds still to open. Look for leaves that are dark green with no sign of yellow.

IN THE GARDEN Sweet Williams are a biennial grown from seed – they take a year to grow and flower after the seeds are sown. Sow in midsummer, either directly or in the greenhouse, in a good alkaline soil in full sun, transplanting them to their final position in the autumn. They will be in flower the following summer.

CONDITIONING Trim the stems between the nodes (these look like joints) and remove any leaves that fall below the surface of the water.

DISPLAY The rich pinks and purples look wonderful with acid-greens. Varieties with an eye (a circular patch of contrasting colour in the centre of the flowers) make a great filler for large blousier flowers and create a real pop in an arrangement.

CARE Refresh the water every 2 days.

Easy to grow from seed, sweet Williams are often better quality home grown or locally purchased.

Foxglove

Digitalis

Foxgloves' tall stems are lined with bell-shaped flowers, each with the most exquisite freckling inside.

Foxgloves effortlessly naturalize into an arrangement, evoking both woodland glades and cottage gardens due to their association with wildflowers. Cultivated varieties come in a range of pinks, purples, and whites, and are the perfect scale and form for large impactful arrangements. For best effect, combine them with other woodland and hedgerow plants.

STEM HEIGHT
1–2m (3–6½ft)

FLOWER SIZE
to 6cm (2½in)

LONGEVITY 10–14 days

FORM spike of bell-shaped flowers

COLOURS purple, pink, white, red, yellow, orange

FRAGRANCE none

BEST COMPANIONS alliums, ammi, peonies, guelder rose

FROM THE FLORIST Select stems that have one third of the bottom bells open, with the rest in bud. The top buds should still be tightly closed.

IN THE GARDEN Foxgloves are a biennial or short-lived perennial grown from seed. Plant in partial shade. They will self-seed and return year after year.

CONDITIONING Remove the lower leaves and cut the dense, thick stems under water to prevent them getting blocked by air bubbles.

DISPLAY These vertical spires associate well with globe shapes, such as peonies, and umbel shapes, such as ammi. Make the most of their stature by arranging them in enamel buckets or large jugs.

CARE Recut the stems and refresh the water every 2 days. If kept cool, they have a relatively long vase life of 10–14 days.

In the language
of flowers, foxgloves
represent insincerity.

Digitalis purpurea '**Camelot**
Lavender', *unlike many varieties,*
flowers in both its first and second
years of growth.

Gypsophila

Gypsophila

Gypsophila stems bear a myriad of tiny flowers, creating fluffy clouds of white or pink.

Gypsophila has both annual and perennial forms. The annual, *G. elegans*, smells sweeter, and has shorter, less rigid stems with single flowers that are larger than those of the perennial. The perennial, *G. paniculata*, bears double flowers, is better known, and is much loved by florists – part of its appeal is its versatility and longevity when out of water.

STEM HEIGHT
G. elegans, to 60cm (24in);
G. paniculata, to 1.2m (4ft)

FLOWER SIZE 1–1.5cm
(½–⅝in)

LONGEVITY
G. elegans, 5 days;
G. paniculata, 10 days

FORMS single, double

COLOURS white, pink

FRAGRANCE
G. paniculata is musty;
G. elegans is honey-like,
particularly 'Deeprose'.

BEST COMPANIONS
roses, sweet peas, lilies

FROM THE FLORIST Make sure the florets are not dry or shrivelled, and that the leaves look fresh.

IN THE GARDEN Gypsophila's annual form, *G. elegans*, is easy to grow from a direct sowing. Sow in succession for prolonged flower production as they only have a 2–3 week flowering period. The perennial form, *G. paniculata*, needs full sun, and lots of water and feed. Harvest the stems when a third of the florets are open.

CONDITIONING Recut the stems and place them in hot tap water to encourage the remaining buds to open. Adding floral preservative to the water will increase the vase life.

DISPLAY Gypsophila is known for its ability to create volume without density, so can be used as a filler in mixed compositions. It also works well arranged on its own to create a big fluffy cloud. The perennial varieties hold well out of water, and can also be dried.

CARE Top up the water every 2 days and the stems should last for a week. The perennial form has more longevity than the annual.

In the language of flowers, gypsophila is a symbol of love, purity, and innocence.

***Gypsophila elegans* 'Deeprose'** *is an annual variety, meaning it dies off each year and must be re-sown.*

"Iris" is the Greek word for rainbow.

Iris siberica is the Latin name for Siberian irises. This variety is called 'Sparkling Rose'.

Iris

Iris

Iris's elegant form and limitless range of colours make it a special cut flower.

Despite there being many different forms of iris, each has three upright petals, which are called "standards", and three draping petals, known as "falls". Bearded, Dutch, and Siberian irises are the three main types used for arranging. Bearded and Siberian irises often have multi- or different coloured petals, while Dutch irises are generally only a single colour.

STEM HEIGHT 0.2–2m (4–72in), depending on variety; *I. siberica*, 30–120cm (12–48in)

FLOWER SIZE 2.5–25cm (1–10in), depending on variety; *I. siberica*, 6–7cm (2½–2¾in)

LONGEVITY 3–10 days, depending on variety

FORMS multiple, such as bearded, Dutch, Siberian, crested

COLOURS purple, pink, blue, yellow, orange, red, brown, white

FRAGRANCE none; bearded have a very sweet scent

BEST COMPANIONS alliums, hesperis, Icelandic poppies

FROM THE FLORIST Choose irises in bud as the petals are fragile and bruise easily. Dutch and Siberian varieties should have flowers emerging from the bud (or "sheath"), but with unseparated falls and standards.

IN THE GARDEN Plant bearded iris rhizomes on small ridges in summer, angling their leaves for maximum sunlight. Ensure the centre of the rhizome is above the soil. Bearded iris should be lifted and divided every 3 years for best flower production. Dutch Iris bulbs are planted in autumn three times their height deep in the soil. They will clump up and produce more flowering stems each year.

CONDITIONING Cut stems at an angle and stand in deep water overnight after cutting.

DISPLAY Irises' intricate form, petal colour, and markings means they are a work of art arranged on their own. If combined with other flowers, go for a contrasting shape; globe-, daisy-, or umbel-shaped flowers work well.

CARE Remove faded flowers and the buds will continue to emerge. Individual flowers will only last 3 days, but the entire stem will last up to 10 days.

Ikebana Irises

I have taken my inspiration from the Japanese art of flower arranging known as "Ikebana", a disciplined and highly regarded art form that acts as a creative expression of nature.

YOU WILL NEED

12 irises (Iris sibirica 'Flight of Butterflies')

copper, footed bowl

large, round pin holder

floral tack

floral snips

ARRANGE

1 Fix the pin holder into the centre of the bowl using floral tack and fill the bowl to the brim with water.

2 Cut the iris stems to around five times the height of the vessel. Push the first two irises into the centre of the pin holder so that they remain fairly upright. Give each flower a bit of space so you can see between their slender stems.

3 To create a crescent-shaped outline, hold up each of the remaining irises to the arrangement to judge position and height before cutting and placing them.

CARE

Top up the water every day. Siberian Irises have a very short vase life of 3 days.

I have tried to symbolize iris's natural habitat growing at the water's edge by using a shallow, footed bowl filled with water.

Sweet Pea

Lathyrus odoratus

Combining fragrance and nostalgia, sweet peas are an enduring favourite.

Sweet peas were one of the first flowers I grew for cutting, and I did so for their intense, sweet scent – something I can never get enough of. These fragrant flowers also appeal because of their prolific, ruffled blooms that come in a wide range of colours and continue to replenish themselves throughout the flowering season.

STEM HEIGHT
to 1.5m (5ft)

FLOWER SIZE
to 3.5cm (1⅜in)

LONGEVITY 3–5 days

FORM clusters of frilly flowers

COLOURS purple, blue, orange, red, pink, white

FRAGRANCE
strong and sweet

BEST COMPANIONS
ammi, peonies, roses

FROM THE FLORIST Look for stems that have two or three of the bottom florets open, and some good-sized buds ready to open at the top.

IN THE GARDEN Sow the seeds in autumn or late winter as these hardy annuals prefer cool conditions while in the seedling stage. Plant out in mid-spring, with supports for the plants to climb up – either canes or netting works well for this. Keep well watered as they grow, tying in the new growth to the supporting structure. Once they start to bloom, just keep picking and the flowers will continue to replenish themselves.

PREPARATION Trim the ends of the stems and condition them overnight in water.

DISPLAY Sweet peas are versatile cut flowers. They look good standing alone in a simple jug or jar, but also work well as a frilly filler in mixed compositions.

CARE The flowers will last longer if arranged on their own as they are sensitive to hormones released by other flowers. The water is unlikely to need topping up during their short vase life.

In the language of flowers,
sweet peas are associated
with fond farewells.

Lathyrus odoratus '**Winter
Sunshine Mid Blue**' *is part of the*
Winter Sunshine *series of cultivars –
a particularly vigorous group that can
be found in a variety of colours.*

Sweet Clusters

I chose to focus on the range of varieties by displaying ten stems of each in different jars. Clustering different coloured varieties in several of the same type of vessel works well for a simple and effective display.

YOU WILL NEED

10 blue sweet pea stems (Lathyrus odoratus 'Winter Sunshine Mid Blue')

10 white sweet pea stems (Lathyrus odoratus 'Oban Bay')

10 purple sweet pea stems (Lathyrus odoratus 'Oyama Bicolour')

3 jars of different sizes

floral snips

ARRANGE

1 Pick a different-sized jar for each variety. Then cut some of each variety so that the flowers sit on the rim of the chosen jar, and the rest between two and three times the height of that jar.

2 Place the stems in the jar, rotating the jar as you do this and angling the outer stems to create a soft, irregular, cloud-like shape.

CARE

Position the jars out of direct sunlight. Sweet peas are sensitive to other plants so keep them away from other flowers and fruit. They arrangement will last for 3–5 days.

For a change in texture and form, try adding some of the sweet peas' tendrils to each jar.

Lavender has been used to cleanse, perfume, and annoint since Ancient Egyptian times.

Lavandula angustifolia is sometimes known as "English lavender", though it is actually native to France, Spain, Italy, and Croatia. This variety is called 'Imperial Gem'.

Lavender

Lavandula

The fragrant purple flower spikes of lavender are a real sensory treat.

Lavender is widely grown for drying, but it also makes a good fresh flower. The soothing and evocative scent is enjoyed in cooking and crafts as well as floristry. I remember cutting lavender with my grandmother, drying the flowers to make lavender bags; I now repeat this ritual with my niece.

STEM HEIGHT
to 50cm (20in)

FLOWER HEAD SIZE
to 8cm (3in)

LONGEVITY 10 days
in water; longer if dried

FORM spike of
tiny flowers

COLOURS purple, blue,
pink, white

FRAGRANCE sweet,
floral, and herbal

BEST COMPANIONS
roses, scabious, nigella

FROM THE FLORIST Lavender should be picked or cut with only a few open florets on the stem. They can also be dried at this stage.

IN THE GARDEN Lavender likes to be in full sun on well-drained alkaline soil. Harvest the flowering stems and give the plants a light trim in late summer. Prune again in early spring to keep the plants compact.

CONDITIONING To preserve the scent, the stems can be dried. Hang bunches of stems in a dark, dry room with plenty of air circulation for 2 weeks.

DISPLAY To create impact, bunch a few stems together and work them into an arrangement as a group.

CARE If you are using a glass vase, change the water every day as it discolours very quickly.

Lily

Lilium

One of the first flowers to be used in floristry, the lily has an exotic air.

Of the nine divisions of lilies, Asiatic hybrids and Oriental hybrids are the most commonly used in floristry. Most are grown in vast greenhouses under carefully controlled conditions to produce long stems and pristine blooms. They are available in almost every colour except blue, and some have spots, stripes, or contrasting colours in the centre.

STEM HEIGHT 1–2m (3–6½ft); *L.* 'Tiger Babies', to 1.2m (3–4ft)

FLOWER SIZE 5–10cm (2–4in); *L.* 'Tiger Babies', 5–7cm (2–2¾in)

LONGEVITY 2 weeks

FORMS multiple, such as Asiatic, Martagon, Candidum, American, Oriental hybrids

FRAGRANCE Oriental hybrids have a strong, heady, exotic perfume

BEST COMPANIONS roses, gypsophila, sweet peas

FROM THE FLORIST Choose stems with the bottom flower just opening and with the next two or three buds full and showing good colour.

IN THE GARDEN Plant the bulbs in full sun and well-drained soil, adding grit if the soil is heavy. Depending on the variety, planting should be done in early autumn or spring. When harvesting lilies, leave enough stem and foliage for photosynthesis and food storage to sustain the bulb until the following season.

CONDITIONING Remove the pollen sacs from the centre of the flower to prevent the pollen staining your clothes. Cut the stems and condition them in water overnight. Lilies do not like floral preservative.

DISPLAY Lilies look excellent on their own so that their curly, reflexed petals and exotic markings can be appreciated without distraction. Their stiff, unwieldy character can make them difficult to place in mixed compositions. However, after some experimentation, I have started to use just one or two stems in more relaxed, garden-gathered arrangements.

CARE Clean the water every 2–3 days and the stems should keep flowering for up to 2 weeks.

Lilium **'Tiger Babies'** *is an Asiatic hybrid. It is scent free, but bears beautiful soft, peach flowers freckled with chocolate-brown spots.*

In Greek mythology, the lily
was the symbol of the goddess
Hera, and was associated with
innocence and purity.

Crouching Tigers

Lily stems are not the easiest flowers to arrange in
a natural style because they are quite stiff and unyielding.
I decided to make the most of their rigidity by placing
them almost horizontally to create a low, wide outline.
The softer, more flexible, frilly and frothy flowers were
then worked in around them.

YOU WILL NEED

2 lily stems
(Lilium 'Tiger Babies')

5 sweet pea stems with
tendrils (Lathyrus odoratus
'Spring Sunshine Burgundy')

3 gyposphila stems
(Gyposphila elegans 'Rosea')

5 roses (Rosa 'Just Joey')

medium-sized, round,
stoneware pot

chicken wire

pot tape

floral snips

ARRANGE

1 Push a chicken-wire ball into the pot, securing with
a cross of pot tape. Then fill the pot with water.

2 Cut the lily stems to about three times the height of
the pot. Position them opposite each other at a sharp,
almost horizontal angle – these will define the shape
of the arrangement.

3 Nestle the roses in the middle of the arrangement.
Hold them up to the pot to judge position and stem
length before cutting and placing. The stems will need
to be cut relatively short.

4 Cut the sweet pea stems to a similar length to the
lily stems (around three times the height of the pot)
and slip them between the lilies and roses.

5 Use the gypsophila to create some frothy fill in
between the lily stems, holding up the stems to the
arrangement to judge position and length.

CARE

Replenish the water every 2 days. The sweet peas,
roses, and gypsophila will finish after 3–5 days, but
the lilies will continue for another 10 days. Either
replace the wilting flowers, or simply remove them
to enjoy the stark beauty of the lilies by themselves.

Stock

Matthiola incana

Best known for their scent, stocks have been grown as a cut flower since the 19th century.

Stocks' stems are densely covered in slightly ruffled florets that give them a plump appearance, and their heady fragrance can fill a room. Although most varieties come in soft and muted colours, they can also be found in shades of wine-red. If growing your own, you can also enjoy the light, airy, single forms selected out by commercial growers.

STEM HEIGHT
to 80cm (32in)

FLOWER HEAD SIZE
to 10cm (4in)

LONGEVITY 5–7 days

FORM spike of single or double flowers

COLOURS pink, purple, blue, yellow, red, white

FRAGRANCE strong, spicy, clove-like

BEST COMPANIONS
peonies, sweet Williams, sweet peas

FROM THE FLORIST Choose stems that have one-third to half of the buds open, and the rest showing good colour.

IN THE GARDEN Sow stock seeds in a greenhouse in late winter or early spring. Prick out and grow on the double form seedlings. Plants only produce one flower each, so plant closely at 10cm (4in) apart in well-prepared fertile soil. Most varieties are best grown under cover.

CONDITIONING Remove any leaves that will be below the surface of the water and cut away any of the thick white fibrous base.

DISPLAY Stocks' dense columns are excellent fillers in blousy arrangements. Their soft, muted colours and spicy fragrance make them a desirable wedding flower, and their spike shape is a perfect partner for globe-shaped flowers.

CARE The water is quickly contaminated by the furry stems, so to prolong the vase life refresh the water daily and recut the stems at an angle.

Matthiola incana cultivars are grown as annuals or biennials, though the species itself is grown as a perennial or small shrub. This cultivar is 'Katz Apricot'.

In the language of flowers, stocks symbolize lasting beauty.

Nigella's flowers change shape
as they develop into seed pods – use
this variety in form to add interest
to arrangements.

Nigella

Nigella

Nigella's ruff of foliage creates a spiky structure around the flowers.

Known as "love-in-a-mist", nigella is grown for both its flowers and decorative, often striped seedpods, the latter developing soon after the petals have faded. Nigella can be found in a number of colours, ranging from white to blue and pink. There are single and semi-double forms available, the semi-doubles having more petals.

STEM HEIGHT
20–75cm (8–30in), depending on variety; *N. damascena*, to 50cm (20in)

FLOWER SIZE 3.5–6cm (1⅜–2½in), depending on variety; *N. damascena*, to 4.5cm (1¾in)

LONGEVITY 7 days

FORMS single and semi-double; *N. hispanica* has a distinctive black seed pod

COLOURS blue, violet, red, pink, white

FRAGRANCE none

BEST COMPANIONS sweet peas, roses, herbs

FROM THE FLORIST Buds that are showing colour will open in the vase. Avoid choosing faded flowers, as these will drop very quickly.

IN THE GARDEN Nigella are hardy annuals grown easily from seed. They are not fussy about soil, but a bit of care will reward you with longer stems and larger flowers. They have a very brief flowering period of two weeks, so sow the seeds both in spring and early autumn to prolong the harvesting time.

CONDITIONING Strip the stems of their feathery foliage, then cut them at an angle and condition overnight in deep water.

DISPLAY Nigella is a diverse cut flower. It can be used as a soft, feathery filler alongside larger-headed, blousy shapes in a romantic bouquet, but it is equally at home in a simple cottage-garden vase or jug. The seed pods are also beautiful to work with, adding contrasting form and texture to mixed compositions.

CARE Buds showing good colour will continue to open in the vase, so refresh the water every 2 days. The petals of the most open flowers will start to shrivel and drop after 7 days.

***Nigella damascena* 'Miss Jekyll Blue'** *has large, sky-blue, semi-double flowers.*

Love-in-a-Mug

The use of a simple mug provides a down-to-earth quality; the roughness of the arrangement's dome-shaped outline adds movement. I have picked nigella at various stages of flowering to enhance the natural, grown-in style.

YOU WILL NEED

*3 rosemary stems
(Rosmarinus officinalis)*

*3 dill stems
(Anethum graveolens)*

*18 nigella flowers and
2 buds (Nigella damascena
'Miss Jekyll White')*

*3 bupleurum stems
(Bupleurum rotundifolium)*

floral snips

hand-thrown mug

ARRANGE

1 Cut the rosemary stems short so that they rest on the rim of the mug. Place them into the mug at equal intervals around the rim.

2 Cut the dill to around twice the height of the mug, positioning it between the rosemary stems.

3 Use the nigella to create a spherical outline for the arrangement. Cut the first four or five stems to around three times the height of the mug and place them in the centre. Hold the remaining stems up to the arrangement to judge position and stem length, and cut and place them appropriately.

4 Fill the base of the arrangement with a few bupleurum stems to add an acid-green pop.

CARE

Top up the water every 2 days and position in a cool place to prolong the vase life – heat will cause the flowers to wilt more quickly.

In Chinese culture, peonies are a symbol of nobility and value, as well as of reproduction and female beauty.

Paeonia lactiflora **'Kansas'** *is a double form – it has more petals than other forms, these creating its rounded shape.*

Peony

Paeonia

The most glamorous of cut flowers, peony's lush, abundant blooms always feel like a decadent treat.

These beautiful flowers come in shades of white, cream, pink, peach, and deep crimson. Their shape ranges from the simple and elegant single form, through to the double form (also known as the "bomb type"). While the strength of their scent varies, at its best it smells like a more delicate lily-of-the-valley.

STEM HEIGHT
0.6–2.5m (2–8ft), depending on variety; *P. lactiflora*, 50–70cm (20–28in)

FLOWER SIZE 5–30cm (2–12in), depending on variety; *P. lactiflora*, 7–10cm (2¾–4in)

LONGEVITY 7–10 days

FORMS single, semi-double, double, anemone-form

COLOURS white, pink, red, yellow

FRAGRANCE sweet, light, lily-of-the-valley-like scent

BEST COMPANIONS alchemilla, sweet peas, sweet Williams

FROM THE FLORIST Select peonies in bud when they are at the "marshmallow" stage (the bud should feel soft and slightly squidgy). If cut when too tight they won't open to their full potential, so do give them a squeeze if you can.

IN THE GARDEN Peony plants normally take 3 years to start flowering but after that need very little attention. They are very hardy, long-lived plants that will bulk up and produce more flowering stems each year. When harvesting, leave about a third of the stems to allow photosynthesis for next year's crop.

CONDITIONING Strip the bottom leaves and cut the stem at a sharp angle. Condition overnight in warm water to encourage them to open.

DISPLAY The flowers are so impressive with their lush, dark green foliage that arranging them by themselves is very satisfying. Choose a low, wide container to accommodate their large heads. Double forms can create a bit of a "clumpy" outline, so break this up with wispy, frilly, or lacy flowers or foliage.

CARE Top up the vase every day, as peonies are thirsty flowers. Refresh the water and clean the vase every 3 days.

Coral and Pink

To make the most of these gorgeous, semi-double, coral-coloured peonies, I used a low, wide vessel – the tarnished surface of this old copper pot contrasts beautifully with the colour and texture of the petals. The acid-green of the foliage and hot-pink of the sweet peas intensifies the peonies' colour to create a vibrant, summery aesthetic.

YOU WILL NEED

5 hornbeam branches (Carpinus betulus)

10 peonies (Paeonia 'Coral Charm')

5 lady's mantle stems (Alchemilla mollis)

7 sweet pea stems (Lathyrus odoratus 'Spring Sunshine Cerise')

chicken wire

copper plant pot

pot tape

secateurs

floral snips

ARRANGE

1 Make a ball of chicken wire and stuff it into the pot so it fits snugly and sits flush with the rim. Secure the top with a cross of tape and fill the pot with water.

2 Cut the hornbeam branches to around two or three times the width of the vessel. Then position two stems horizontally and one vertically to create the outline of the arrangement.

3 Use the peonies to create a soft dome shape. Hold each flower up to the arrangement to judge position and stem length. Cut and place them appropriately, angling the heads to face in different directions.

4 Tuck the lady's mantle and sweet pea stems in amongst the peonies. Make sure the sweet peas extend out from the arrangement to break up the outline of the dome.

CARE

Top up the water every 2 days and replace the sweet peas after around 3–5 days. The peonies will last for 7–10 days, and the lady's mantle up to 2 weeks.

Icelandic poppies grow naturally in cold, subarctic climates. However, despite their name, they are not found in Iceland.

Icelandic Poppy

Papaver nudicaule

Icelandic poppies are some of the most exquisite cut flowers you can find.

Coming in a range of luminescent colours, fragrant Icelandic poppies bridge the gap between spring and summer. Their silky, tissue-like petals have a crinkled appearance as they unfurl from their buds, making them look impossibly fragile when they are in fact surprisingly robust.

STEM HEIGHT to 30cm (12in)

FLOWER SIZE to 8cm (3in)

LONGEVITY 3–5 days

FORMS single, semi-double

COLOURS yellow, orange, red, pink, white

FRAGRANCE strong and soapy

BEST COMPANIONS buttercups, peonies, white laceflowers, quaking grass, sweet peas

FROM THE FLORIST Buy poppies while their stems are still in bud, but with a seam of petal showing.

IN THE GARDEN Icelandic poppies are biennials grown from seed, so sow them a year before they are due to flower. Start off the seeds in trays in the greenhouse in early to midsummer, transferring them to their final planting position in autumn. Keep picking and deadheading so they will flower for up to 6 weeks.

PREPARATION After cutting, sear the stems so that they retain their moisture (see pp.22–23).

DISPLAY Poppies make excellent focal flowers, their bright yellow centres drawing in the eye. They combine well with grasses and umbel-shaped flowers to create meadow-style arrangements, but are also happy jostling amongst sweet peas and peonies in hand-tied bouquets or vase-style arrangements.

CARE Refresh the water every 2 days and keep in a cool position. If they are looking floppy, recut and re-sear the stems.

Papaver nudicaule **'Champagne Bubbles'** *are easy to germinate and are available in a good range of colours.*

Spring Meadow Jar

To capture a wild, meadow style, I've combined Icelandic poppies with white laceflower and quaking grass. Less is more with this type of arrangement – you need to create lots of air, imagining pollinating insects winging their way between the flowers.

YOU WILL NEED

15 Icelandic poppies (Papaver nudicaule)

7 white laceflower stems (Orlaya grandiflora)

7 sweet pea stems (Lathyrus odoratus)

10 quaking grass stems (Briza maxima)

medium-sized, straight-edged jar

floral pin holder

floral tack

floral snips

ARRANGE

1 Place the floral pin holder at the bottom of the jar and secure with a floral tack. This will help you to keep the arrangement open as you won't need to add flowers in order to keep the stems in place.

2 First push the poppies into the pins at the bottom of the jar, leaving a good space between the flowers.

3 Fill in the gaps with the laceflowers and sweet peas. Keep some of the laceflower stems lower and at more of an angle in the jar.

4 Slip in the quaking grass stems between the flowers to add delicacy and movement.

CARE

Icelandic poppies and sweet peas have a vase life of 3–5 days, after which the petals will start to drop. The white laceflowers and quaking grass will last 7–10 days, so the arrangement could be refreshed with more poppies and sweet peas. Be sure to refresh the water and sear the stems of the new poppies.

Rose

Rosa

The queen of cut flowers, rose's beauty and scent make it many people's favourite flower.

This quintessentially English flower comes in a staggering range of varieties. It is available in every colour apart from true blue, and its heavenly fragrance is unrivalled. The old-fashioned varieties produce a breath-taking display of highly scented flowers in June, whilst modern, repeat-flowering varieties can be productive through until October.

The rose has been used throughout history as a political, artistic, and cultural symbol. Today, it is most commonly associated with love.

STEM HEIGHT 0.3–2m (1–6½ft), depending on variety; *R.* 'Proper Job', to 1.2m (4ft)

FLOWER SIZE 4–15cm (1½–6in), depending on variety; *R.* 'Proper Job', 10cm (4in)

LONGEVITY 3–7 days, depending on the variety; more fragrant roses have a shorter vase life

FORMS multiple, such as flat, rounded, cupped, high-centred, rosette, quartered-rosette

COLOURS pink, red, white, orange, yellow, green

FRAGRANCE fragrance varies from "fruity" to "tea"

BEST COMPANIONS sweet peas, herbs, ammi, bellflowers, lavender

FROM THE FLORIST Choose roses with outer petals that are just starting to unfurl. The centre should still be firm to the touch. Check that no petals have been removed from the flower's base.

IN THE GARDEN Roses are best planted in the dormant season (during winter) as bare-root plants rather than in containers. They are hungry and thirsty plants, so to gain cut-flower-quality blooms they need plenty of feeding and watering. Regular deadheading will encourage repeat flowering, and prune them hard in late winter to encourage vigorous, tall regrowth.

CONDITIONING Cut the stems at a sharp angle and sear them (see pp.22–23). Then place them in tepid water overnight.

DISPLAY Roses are one of my favourite flowers to arrange – the soft, relaxed character of garden varieties makes them incredibly versatile focal flowers. Combine different varieties to show off their contrasting shapes. I tend to use harmonious colours, but you may want to explore different combinations. Select a range of flowering stages for further variation.

CARE Top up the water every 2 days. Recut and re-sear the stems if the flowers start to look soft.

Rosa 'Proper Job' *has a quartered-rosette form that is often referred to as "an old-fashioned rose".*

Harmonious Roses

This is an abundant, voluptuous design honouring the garden rose – its scale possible because of the punch-bowl container. To relish this flower in all of its glory, I included as many varieties as possible in harmonious colours.

YOU WILL NEED

3 hornbeam branches
(Carpinus betulus)

3 berried guelder rose stems
(Viburnum opulus)

14 roses of different cultivars
(Rosa 'Chris Beardshaw', R. 'Commonwealth Glory', R. 'Duchess of Cornwall', R. 'Moody Blue', R. 'A Whiter Shade of Pale')

5 milky bellflower stems
(Campanula lactiflora)

5 astrantia stems
(Astrantia major)

3 jasmine stems
(Jasminum officinalis)

3 Chinese forget-me-not stems (Cynoglossum amabile)

2 red-leaved rose stems
(Rosa glauca)

1 rambling rose stem
(Rosa 'Wedding Day')

silver punch bowl

chicken wire

pot tape

secateurs

ARRANGE

1 Place a large ball of chicken wire into the bowl – it should be big enough to touch the edges – securing with a cross of pot tape. Then fill the bowl with water.

2 Use the hornbeam branches to create a framework for the arrangement. They should be around two to three times the height of the container.

3 Cut the guelder rose stems to around one-and-a-half times the height of the container and use them to fill in the front and sides of the arrangement.

4 Fill the arrangement with roses. Hold them up to the vase to judge position and stem length before cutting and placing appropriately. Cut the large blooms shorter and nestle them into the foliage. Place smaller roses with branching stems along the lines of foliage.

5 Place the milky bellflower and astrantia in the gaps between the roses.

6 Add long lengths of jasmine, Chinese forget-me-nots, red-leaved rose, and rambling rose. Angle some vertically above the roses and trail others down towards the table.

CARE

Keep in a cool position to prolong the vase life of the roses and top up the water daily. The most fragrant roses will start to drop after 3 days, but others will last up to 7 days.

Guelder Rose

— Viburnum opulus —

These pom-pom-shaped, apple-green blooms provide a wonderful backdrop for other spring flowers.

I think of guelder rose as the spring-flowering equivalent of hydrangeas – the round clusters of flowers look very similar, especially as they age. Guelder rose's tall, branching stems, soft-green flowers, and indented foliage are perfect for large-scale arrangements, creating a good foundation into which other flowers can be worked.

STEM HEIGHT cut branches to desired length

FLOWER HEAD SIZE to 8cm (3in)

LONGEVITY 7–14 days

FORM round clusters of small flowers

COLOURS green, white

FRAGRANCE none

BEST COMPANIONS Icelandic poppies, sweet peas, alliums

FROM THE FLORIST Choose stems with a good green colour, and that are dense and firm to the touch. The flowers become larger, softer, and whiter as they age.

IN THE GARDEN This fast-growing shrub is easy to grow and is happy in most positions and soil types. It has a short flowering season (only 2 weeks), so make the most of the harvest and prune after flowering.

CONDITIONING Cut a cross in the woody stems and sear the stem end (see pp.22–23).

DISPLAY The soft, green flowers beautifully balance rich, vibrant colours and lift soft, muted ones. I like to combine them with spire-, daisy-, umbel-, and other ball-shaped flowers in a large jug or vase.

CARE If flowers and leaves start to droop, re-cut and sear the stems.

Viburnum opulus 'Roseum' *is known as "snowball tree".*

The berries that follow guelder rose's flowers can also be used as a filler or final flourish.

LATE SUMMER & AUTUMN

Achillea millefolium 'Summer Pastels' *is a short-lived perennial that is easily grown from seed in a wide range of pastel colours.*

Yarrow

Achillea

Yarrow's colour palette reminds me of a Persian carpet, with deep reds and pinks to golden yellow.

Yarrow produces flat-topped or slightly domed flower heads. These emerge on branching stems above clumps of fern-textured foliage. The flower heads are made up of hundreds of florets that look like tiny daisies. As they age they fade and their colours become softer and more muted.

In Greek mythology, Achilles used yarrow to treat the wounds of his soldiers. This is why its botanical name is *Achillea*.

STEM/BRANCH HEIGHT 30–80cm (12–32in), depending on variety; *A. millefolium*, to 60cm (24in)

FLOWER HEAD SIZE 5–12cm (2–4¾in), depending on variety; *A. millefolium*, 7–10cm (2¾–4in)

LONGEVITY 7–14 days

FORMS flat-topped or domed clusters of small flowers

COLOURS red, orange, yellow, pink, white

FRAGRANCE sharp and herbal

BEST COMPANIONS grasses, scabious, sea holly

FROM THE FLORIST Choose stems with brightly coloured florets that are fully open. Check the foliage looks fresh, as shrivelled stem foliage indicates that the plant has been in storage for too long.

IN THE GARDEN It enjoys a sunny position and does not mind poor soil, as long as it is not too wet. Although it is a perennial plant, I treat it as an annual, replacing the plants every year or two. It can also be lifted and divided in the spring or autumn.

CONDITIONING Strip the stem foliage, cut at a sharp angle, and condition overnight in water. Handle with gloves if you have sensitive skin, as the plant can be irritant.

DISPLAY A great filler flower for late summer and autumn arrangements, yarrow's warm colours suit the time of year and it is perfect for naturalizing mixed compositions. The stems can also be air-dried for winter work by hanging them upside down in a well-ventilated space.

CARE Refresh the water every 2 days.

Love-lies-bleeding is associated with eternity due to its long flowering period.

Amaranthus caudatus **'Coral Fountain'** *is a half-hardy annual with drooping tassels of soft, coral flowers.*

Love-Lies-Bleeding

Amaranthus caudatus

Love-lies-bleeding's shape and texture make it a dramatic addition to summer arrangements.

Love-lies-bleeding has draping panicles that are similar in texture to chenille fabric. This half-hardy annual comes in a range of colours and keeps its cascade of velvet tassels or spikes well into autumn. It can also be dried and used for winter wreaths and garlands.

STEM HEIGHT
1–1.5m (3–5ft)

FLOWER HEAD SIZE
45–60cm (18–24in)

LONGEVITY 7–10 days

FORMS drooping spikes of tiny flowers

COLOURS red, brown, green

FRAGRANCE none

BEST COMPANIONS
dahlias, sunflowers, hypericum berries

FROM THE FLORIST Check that the flower stems are not limp, and that the leaves are still looking fresh.

IN THE GARDEN Love-lies-bleeding is easy to grow from seed, started indoors in spring and then planted out in a sunny position after the last frosts. Start to pick when the tassels begin to form and before the tiny seeds start to drop. Keep picking and watering to prolong the flowering period.

CONDITIONING Remove most of the leaves to reveal the tassel-like flowers. Then sear the stems (see pp.22–23) before putting them in deep water overnight to condition.

DISPLAY Love-lies-bleeding's scale and drama demand bold, large-scale arrangements to accommodate the draping stems, which look wonderful in large footed vessels where the tassels can cascade down the sides.

CARE Top up the water every 2–3 days. If the stems look floppy, recut and re-sear them.

When squeezed, snapdragon's flowers appear to open and close like a mouth – hence its common name. However, its botanical name means "nose-like" in Greek.

Antirrhinum majus '**Madame Butterfly**' *is a half-hardy annual with large, double flowers.*

Snapdragon

Antirrhinum majus

A garden favourite, snapdragons have statuesque stems lined with velvety flowers.

The snapdragon is what I call "a happy flower". It comes in an amazing range of vivid colours and even bi-colours, and its scent reminds me of an old-fashioned sweet shop. Snapdragons flower for months – from the first statuesque cut of the primary stem in high summer, to the quirky, kinky stems that appear in autumn.

STEM HEIGHT
0.25–2m (¾–6½ft);
A. majus 'Madame
Butterfly', 75cm (30in)

FLOWER SIZE
3–4.5cm (1¼–1¾in)

LONGEVITY 10 days

FORMS single, double

COLOURS pink, purple,
red, orange, yellow, cream,
white

FRAGRANCE light, fruity

BEST COMPANIONS
ammi, dahlias, berries

FROM THE FLORIST Choose stems that have a third to a half of the florets open. Avoid those where the lower florets are dropping.

IN THE GARDEN Snapdragons are half-hardy perennials that are generally grown from seed as annuals. Sow indoors in early spring and plant outside once the risk of frost has passed. Pinch out the tips when planting to encourage the plants to become bushy, with multiple flowering stems. Once they start to flower, keep picking and they will continue to flower for months.

CONDITIONING Strip the bottom leaves and condition overnight. Try to keep the stems upright in the bucket if you want them to stay straight.

DISPLAY The larger-stemmed flowers are perfect for bold, statement-piece arrangements such as pedestals, while the smaller stems add a feathery outline to bouquets.

CARE Buds will continue to open in the vase, but will be slightly paler in colour than those that have opened before being cut. Keep the water clean by refreshing it every 2–3 days.

Sherbet Snapdragons

Snapdragons' tall spire shapes naturally fit a tall, narrow container. However, I decided to go the other way by selecting a low, wide jar that would create a symmetrical fan of spires with plenty of air and light in between.

YOU WILL NEED

5 bupleurum stems
(Bupleurum rotundifolium)

7 ammi stems
(Ammi majus 'Snowflake')

1 feverfew stem
(Tanacetum parthenium)

15 snapdragon stems
(Antirrhinum majus
'Sherbet Toned
Chantilly Mix')

wide glass jar

clear, waterproof tape

floral snips

ARRANGE

1 Fill the jar with water, then make a lattice over the opening at the top using clear tape (see pp.14–15).

2 Cut the bupleurum so that its stems can rest at a sharp angle around the rim of the jar. Use its flowers to create the outline of your fan shape.

3 Cut the ammi stems to around two to three times the height of the container. Use them as filler foliage to fill the area above the jar, maintaining the shape of the arrangement.

4 Cut the feverfew short (around one to two times the height of the jar). Nestle it in amongst the green foliage to create a "carpet of daisies".

5 Cut the snapdragons to varying lengths between two and three times the height of the container. Hold them up to the arrangement to judge the required position and length. Scatter them throughout the other flowers, resting them on the other plants so their weight is supported.

CARE

Refresh the water every 2–3 days, removing any dropped flowers. The arrangement will last up to 10 days.

Aster

Various genera

This unpretentious garden stalwart adds colour and frothy texture to autumn bouquets.

The genus *Aster* has recently been divided into several smaller genera, although many have retained the common name aster. A hardy perennial that bears a froth of small, single or double daisies on multi-branched stems, aster flowers well into the autumn months. The blooms attract pollinating insects, and bring life and colour to end-of-season arrangements.

STEM HEIGHT 30–150cm (1–5ft), depending on variety; *S. novae-angliae*, 1.2–1.5m (4–5ft)

FLOWER SIZE 1–8cm (⅝–3in), depending on variety; *S. novae-angliae*, to 5cm (2in)

LONGEVITY 10–14 days

FORMS single, double

COLOURS pink, purple, blue, white

FRAGRANCE none

BEST COMPANIONS chrysanthemums, dahlias, love-lies-bleeding

FROM THE FLORIST Check the lower stems for brown or decayed leaves. The centres of the flowers should be a bright yellow and there should be four or five flowers open on each branch.

IN THE GARDEN Aster will grow in full sun or partial shade. Some varieties are prone to mildew, but a moisture-retentive soil will help prevent this. Cut back in the early spring and divide every 3 years to keep plants flowering well.

CONDITIONING Strip the lower leaves and cut the stems at a sharp angle, before conditioning overnight.

DISPLAY Aster is an invaluable frothy filler for autumnal displays. The rich pinks and purples match the season's palette well, and it provides volume and texture amongst larger, bolder focal flowers.

CARE Refresh the water every 2–3 days to maximize the plant's vase life.

In the language of flowers, asters are a symbol of patience.

Symphyotrichum novae-angliae **'Violetta'** *is a hardy variety commonly referred to as New England aster.*

Briza maxima is native to
southern Europe, North
Africa, and western Asia.

Quaking Grass

Briza

Quaking grass's elegant, hanging seedheads are animated by the slightest of breezes.

In the language of flowers, grass is a symbol of submission.

Although there are several varieties available, I tend to use the largest, greater quaking grass (*B. maxima*). This form has silver-green seedheads that are shaped like scaly, heart-shaped lockets and turn golden as the summer progresses.

STEM HEIGHT 45–60cm (18–24in)

SEEDHEAD SIZE to 1cm (½in)

LONGEVITY 10–14 days in water; longer if dried

FORMS greater, common, lesser

COLOURS green, golden

FRAGRANCE none

BEST COMPANIONS Icelandic poppies, nigella, zinnias

FROM THE FLORIST Look for a good, silver-green colour and tight seedheads.

IN THE GARDEN A hardy annual grass, quaking grass is best sown from seed directly in autumn or spring, and then thinned out. It will take some shade and a richer soil than most grasses. I like planting it in pots to decorate outdoor tables.

CONDITIONING Trim the ends and carefully place in water overnight, ensuring that the stems do not become tangled.

DISPLAY Like most grasses, quaking grass adds movement and elegance to arrangements, and is the perfect final flourish. It also dries very well if harvested as it is turning golden, but if cut and dried before this point, it starts breaking up. To dry, bunch and hang the stems upside down in a cool, dark place.

CARE Grasses are always long lived in an arrangement. Check the water level every 3–4 days and they will age and dry gracefully in the vase.

Chrysanthemum

Chrysanthemum

Primarily a striking focal flower, chrysanthemum's diversity makes it a versatile flower to arrange.

Chrysanthemums come in a huge variety of shapes and sizes, separated into ten categories depending on the form. Florists' chrysanthemums generally have either one large flower head per stem (disbudded stems), or multiple smaller flower heads (spray stems). Both groups have early and late flowering varieties, so they are available from late summer through to winter.

STEM LENGTH
20–200cm (8–78in), depending on variety; C. 'Fuego Bronze', to 70cm (28in)

FLOWER HEAD SIZE
2.5–30cm (1–12in), depending on variety; C. 'Fuego Bronze', to 10cm (4in)

LONGEVITY
2 weeks

FORMS multiple, such as single, incurved, intermediate, reflexed, fully reflexed, pompon

COLOURS pink, purple, red, orange, yellow, white, green

FRAGRANCE musky

BEST COMPANIONS dahlias, hypericum berries, roses

FROM THE FLORIST Choose stems with fully open flowers as they do not open once cut.

IN THE GARDEN Chrysanthemum is an easy plant to grow. Plant in an open, sunny position with well-drained soil. Some varieties are designed for indoor cultivation and, if given protection from frosts, will continue flowering until midwinter. Other hardier varieties will do well outside, as long as they are supported and sheltered from winds. Pests can prove an issue. Regular feeding and bud removal will produce quality flowers for cutting.

CONDITIONING Cut the stems at a sharp angle and remove any leaves that would be under water.

DISPLAY Disbudded stems provide the perfect focal flower for autumnal displays, while spray stems and pompon (or button) forms work best as a filler.

CARE Chrysanthemums are renowned for their long vase life – refresh the water every 2–3 days and they will happily last for 2 weeks. Chrysanthemums release hormones that shorten the vase life of other flowers. Replace other flowers to increase longevity of chrysanthemum arrangements.

Chrysanthemums are grown as competition flowers by amateur and professional flower growers alike.

Chrysanthemum 'Fuego Bronze' *has an intermediate form with two-tone florets.*

Copper & Bronze

These showy, bronze-toned chrysanthemums are the epitome of autumn. I decided to maximize this seasonality with an old copper pot and plenty of hedgerow-foraged branches and berries. The wide shape of the pot coupled with the scale of the flower heads and foliage led me to create a low, wide arrangement.

YOU WILL NEED

*5 eucalyptus stems
(Eucalyptus gunnii)*

*4 berried viburnum stems
(Viburnum opulus)*

*2 hawthorn branches
(Crataegus monogyna)*

*2 red-leaved rose branches
(Rosa glauca)*

*8 chrysanthemums
(Chrysanthemum 'Fuego
Bronze')*

*4 great burnet stems
(Sanguisorba officinalis)*

*3 strawflowers
(Xerochrysum bracteatum)*

*6 zinnias
(Zinnia 'Jazzy Mix')*

round, copper flower pot

chicken wire

pot tape

floral snips

secateurs

ARRANGE

1 Place a chicken-wire ball inside the pot. Secure it with a cross of pot tape and fill the container three-quarters full of water.

2 Cut the eucalyptus so that it is about twice the width of the pot and position into the arrangement at various angles – some should be upright, others horizontal or draped over the side.

3 Cut the viburnum stems short and use them to fill in the centre and at the front. Cut the hawthorn and red-leaved rose to three times the width of the pot. Place them so they stretch out beyond the eucalyptus.

4 Cut the chrysanthemums' stems quite short, so that only the flowers are visible when are they positioned in among the foliage. Angle some towards the back and side for a natural look.

5 Leave the stems of the great burnet, strawflowers, and zinnias long, and nestle them in amongst the chrysanthemums so that they look like they are hovering above the flowers.

CARE

Top up the water every 2–3 days and the arrangement will last for 7–10 days.

The word cosmos comes
from the Greek word *kosmos*,
meaning "the world".

Cosmos

— *Cosmos* —

Cosmos has an understated elegance with its crinkled petals and open flowers.

Two types of cosmos are used as cut flowers. *C. atrosanguineus* (chocolate cosmos) is readily found in florists and has a chocolate-like colour and scent. *C. bipinnatus* is easy to grow and has delicate, ferny foliage; it produces an abundance of single or semi-double flowers, the semi-doubles having more petals, in a range of whites, pinks, and reds.

C. atrosanguineus is now extinct in the wild. Cultivated plants are widely available, and are all clones of a single original plant.

STEM HEIGHT
C. atrosanguineus, to 75cm (30in); *C. bipinnatus*, to 1.5m (5ft)

FLOWER SIZE
C. atrosanguineus, to 4.5cm (1¾in); *C. bipinnatus*, to 8cm (3in)

LONGEVITY 10 days

FORMS single, semi-double

COLOURS white, pink, red, brown

FRAGRANCE
C. atrosanguineus has a chocolate-like scent

BEST COMPANIONS
ammi, larkspur, scabious

FROM THE FLORIST Choose stems when the first flower is just starting to open and there is no sign of pollen in the centre. *C. bipinnatus* has fragile flowers that do not transport well, so is better when sourced locally.

IN THE GARDEN *C. atrosanguineus* likes a fertile, moist, but well-drained soil, and can be mulched or lifted and stored indoors over winter. *C. bipinnatus* is a half-hardy annual that is grown from seed. Start it in a greenhouse or sow it directly into the soil after the danger of frost has passed. It likes full sun and a moist, but well-drained soil. Deadhead and pick regularly to prolong flowering.

CONDITIONING Strip the lower leaves, then cut the stems at an angle and condition overnight.

DISPLAY *C. atrosanguineus* makes the perfect finishing flourish, appearing to hover above the rest of the flowers on its wiry stem; its maroon colour works with soft and bright colour palettes. *C. bipinnatus* looks beautiful in a simple jug by itself, or as an airy addition to casual, country-style arrangements.

CARE Refresh the water every 2–3 days to encourage the buds to open.

Cosmos Cloud

I chose a simple large jug to enhance the casual style of the design. The beautiful, lacy foliage meant there was no need for other flowers, just a few frothy stems of ammi to complement the cosmos's fragile, daisy-like flowers.

YOU WILL NEED
20 cosmos stems of different varieties (Cosmos bipinnatus 'Fizzy White', C. bipinnatus 'Picotee', C. bipinnatus 'Seashells')

7 ammi stems (Ammi majus 'Snowflake')

floral snips

large turquoise jug

ARRANGE
1 Fill the jug with water, then cut the cosmos stems to around three times the height of the jug.

2 Position the cosmos in the jug to form a round, open shape. Hold the stems up to the arrangement to judge position and stem length before cutting and placing.

3 Fill in any gaps between the cosmos stems with the voluminous ammi stems.

CARE
Top up the water every 2 days. Keep the arrangement in a cool position. It should happily last 7 days.

Combining a few varieties of cosmos en masse creates an arrangement akin to how the plant looks in growth.

Crocosmia

Crocosmia

Natives to South Africa, crocosmia herald high summer with their blaze of hot colours.

Crocosmia, or montbretia, are known for their graceful, arching sprays of brilliantly coloured funnel-shaped flowers, accompanied by emerald green blade-like foliage. The seedheads that appear after flowering are also decorative and dry well. They are one of my favourite flowers to arrange.

STEM/BRANCH HEIGHT 0.6–1.5m (2–5ft), depending on variety; C. 'Lucifer', 1–1.2m (3–4ft)

FLOWER SIZE 2–6cm (¾–2½in), depending on variety; C. 'Lucifer', to 5cm (2in)

LONGEVITY 7 days

FORMS spikes of funnel-shaped flowers

COLOURS red, orange, yellow

FRAGRANCE none

BEST COMPANIONS dill, sea holly, zinnias

FROM THE FLORIST Choose stems that have the first two or three florets open.

IN THE GARDEN Crocosmia are grown from corms (bulbs) that quickly form clumps in well-drained soil. They are slightly tender, so need protection during a cold winter. Lift and divide every 4 years. They will not flourish in poor, dry soil and must have plenty of fertility and moisture to thrive.

CONDITIONING Remove the outer leaves and trim the stems at a sharp angle before conditioning them overnight in water.

DISPLAY Crocosmia's eye-catching colour is tempered by the delicacy of its form. This makes it a very useful addition to mixed compositions needing a pop of colour and a feathery outline. They work especially well with daisy- and umbel-shaped flowers.

CARE Refresh the water every 2–3 days and the buds showing colour may open.

Crocosmia derives from the Greek words *krokos*, meaning "saffron", and *osme*, "odour", referring to the smell of the dried leaves.

Crocosmia 'Lucifer' *has furnace-red, trumpet-like flowers on tall upright stems, and pleated, bright green leaves.*

Dahlia '**Ivanetti**' *is a small member of the ball group of dahlias. It has good stem length and vase life, so is an excellent variety for cutting.*

Dahlia

Dahlia

No other flower is as generous in its variety of colours and forms, or in its prolific flowering.

There are literally hundreds of varieties of dahlias to choose from: they are available in five sizes and ten different forms, and can be found in a breath-taking range of colours. To make selecting varieties for cutting easier, I focus mainly on small and medium sizes, and ball, decorative, and waterlily forms, which all tend to have a longer vase life.

STEM HEIGHT
0.6–1.5m (2–5ft), depending on variety; *D.* 'Ivanetti', to 1.1m (3½ft)

FLOWER SIZE 5–30cm (2–12in), depending on variety; *D.* 'Ivanetti', to 10cm (4in)

LONGEVITY 5–7 days

FORMS multiple, such as single-flowered, waterlily, collerette, pompon, ball, cactus, decorative

COLOURS pink, purple, red, orange, yellow, white

FRAGRANCE none

BEST COMPANIONS ammi, hypericum, grasses

FROM THE FLORIST Check the undersides and reverse of the flowers to ensure none of the petals are soft or discoloured.

IN THE GARDEN Dahlias can be planted in pots in spring, and grown on under cover until after the last frost. Then plant them outside. Dahlias need a sunny position and well-drained soil. They are hungry and thirsty plants that will produce better flowers when given a high-potash feed. Deadhead and pick regularly to prolong flowering, which should go on until the first frosts.

CONDITIONING Cut the hollow stems under water to avoid creating an airblock. Then strip off most of the leaves and condition them overnight in water before arranging.

DISPLAY Definitely a focal flower, dahlias grab all of the attention with their colour and form. They are quite stiff and dense, so I like to put them with flowers and foliage that have plenty of movement and texture, such as umbels, spires, berries, and grasses.

CARE Change the water every 2 days.

In the language of flowers, dahlias are a symbol of dignity.

Dahlias in Pewter

Dahlias come in such an overwhelming range of colours, shapes, and sizes that they need no additional flowers or foliage. I included several varieties in this arrangement by using a cluster of ten different-sized vessels.

YOU WILL NEED
32 dahlias of different cultivars and 9 dahlia buds
(Dahlia 'Alauna Clair Obscur',
D. 'American Dawn',
D. 'Apache Blue',
D. 'Blue Bayou',
D. 'Burlesca',
D. 'Carolina Wagemans',
D. 'Cartouche',
D. 'Classic Poeme',
D. 'Franz Kafka',
D. 'Geerlings Cupido',
D. 'Hamari Rose',
D. 'Karma Fuchsiana',
D. 'Labyrinth',
D. 'Lilac Time',
D. 'Maldiva',
D. 'New Baby',
D. 'Night Butterfly',
D. 'Orfeo',
D. 'Paradise City',
D. 'Peaches',
D. 'Preference',
D. 'Purple Flame',
D. 'Taratahi Ruby',
D. 'Totally Tangerine',
D. 'Uncle Hanky',
D. 'Whitman's Best',
D. 'Who Dun It',
D. 'Worton Blue Streak')

a selection of pewter tankards in different sizes

floral snips

ARRANGE
1 Fill the containers with water and arrange them in a triangle formation.

2 Hold the dahlias up to the arrangement to judge position and stem length before cutting and placing appropriately. Put some of the largest flowers lower down so that they ground the arrangement. Leave the stems of some of the small and medium-sized dahlias long so that their blooms appear to float above the rest of the flowers. You may want to move the containers around as you are arranging.

CARE
Top up the containers with water every 2–3 days and the arrangement should last 5 days.

This arrangement is all about experimentation – try moving flowers to different positions until you are happy.

Sea Holly

Eryngium

Sea holly's thistle-like flowers have a wonderfully architectural quality.

Sea holly comes in a range of colours. The florets are borne plentifully on multi-branched stems, each sitting on a specialized leaf (or "bract"). The smaller varieties, such as *E. planum*, make excellent fillers, while *E. giganteum* can hold its own as a focal flower. The flowers can also be dried.

STEM HEIGHT 0.6–1.5m (2–5ft), depending on variety; *E. giganteum* 'Silver Ghost', to 60m (2ft)

FLOWER HEAD SIZE 4–12cm (1¼–4¾in), depending on variety; *E. giganteum* 'Silver Ghost', 12cm (4¾in)

LONGEVITY 2 weeks in water; longer if dried

FORM near-spherical flower heads with spiky bracts

COLOURS green, blue, purple, silver

FRAGRANCE musty

BEST COMPANIONS milky bellflowers, roses, scabious

FROM THE FLORIST Look for good, rich colour and sheen. Check the bracts are not looking discoloured – a sign that they have been stored too long. A strong, musty smell is also an indication that the flowers are not fresh.

IN THE GARDEN Sea holly needs full sun to reach its best colour. It can tolerate poor soil, but dislikes waterlogging. Some varieties will self-seed.

CONDITIONING Cut stems at an angle and condition them overnight in deep water.

DISPLAY Sea holly's spiky thistles contrast well with softer blooms. The larger, bright silver *E. giganteum* makes an excellent focal flower with its distinctive ruff. *E. planum*, the smaller, blue variety with wiry stems and small thistles, is a good finishing flourish, and looks at home in wildflower-style arrangements beside daisy shapes and grasses.

CARE Refresh the water every 2 days.

Eryngium giganteum **'Silver Ghost'** *is a short-lived perennial with metallic silver leaves and painfully spiky bracts.*

In the language of flowers,
sea holly is a symbol of austerity
and independence.

Sea Holly Bouquet

I included two sizes of sea holly in this hand-tie, the larger
acting as a focal flower and the smaller as a final flourish.
I used harmonious colours that complement the green sea
holly, aiming to create variety through texture and form.

YOU WILL NEED

7 roses (Rosa 'Irish Hope')

*3 milky bellflower stems
(Campanula lactiflora)*

*2 large sea holly flowers
(Eryngium giganteum
'Silver Ghost')*

*12 small sea holly flowers
(Eryngium planum)*

*1 eucalyptus stem
(Eucalyptus gunnii)*

*3 sweet peas
(Lathyrus odoratus)*

*3 pineapple mint stems
(Mentha suaveolens
'Variegata')*

*4 nigella stems (Nigella
hispanica 'Delft Blue')*

*5 triteleia stems
(Triteleia 'Queen Fabiola')*

*2 nigella seed heads
(Nigella damascena)*

*4 hornbeam branches
(Carpinus betulus)*

floral snips

raffia or twine

ARRANGE

For further instructions on how to arrange
a hand-tied bouquet see pp.26–27.

1 Remove all of the leaves and any side shoots from
the bottom two-thirds of each stem. Then lay all of
the material out in piles so that it is easy to select.

2 Take one of the roses and hold it in your wrong
hand between your thumb and forefinger. One by
one, add the flower and foliage stems, experimenting
with which look good next to each other, and trying
different types of material alternately. Save the
hornbeam branches until the end.

3 Add the final few stems from the top, using
the remaining coloured flowers to break up large
areas of green.

4 Now add the hornbeam branches around the
edges. These have woodier stems that will support
and protect the softer stems within the bouquet.

5 Tie the bouquet off with raffia or twine, before
trimming the ends so that the height of the bouquet
is about a hand and a half.

CARE

Hand-tied bouquets do not last more than a few
hours out of water. If you want to revive it, trim the
ends and place in a large jar or jug.

Sunflower

Helianthus annuus

You cannot help but be cheered by the open, sunny face of a sunflower.

The best sunflowers for cutting are the annual, pollen-free cultivars. There are many sizes and colours to choose from, including creams, lemons, golds, and reds, as well as bi-coloured varieties. Plants will often branch willingly if the buds are removed and, if they are picked regularly, will produce flowers for several weeks.

STEM HEIGHT 0.3–5m (1–16ft), depending on variety; *H. annuus*, to 5m (16ft)

FLOWER HEAD SIZE 5–30cm (2–12in), depending on variety; *H. annuus*, to 30cm (12in)

LONGEVITY 7–10 days

FORMS single, double

COLOURS yellow, cream, red

FRAGRANCE none

BEST COMPANIONS love-lies-bleeding, dill, snapdragons

FROM THE FLORIST The centre is the best indication of freshness – there should be no pollen and it should be dark and tight.

IN THE GARDEN Sunflowers are hardy annuals grown from seed. Either sow in pots in a greenhouse in early spring, or directly into the ground in mid- to late spring once the weather is warmer. Give them plenty of space – they should be about 45cm (18in) apart. Pinch out the tops when they are about 20cm (8in) high to encourage branching and lots of smaller, more useable flowers.

CONDITIONING Remove all foliage from the stem – it is not as long lasting as the flowers and will make the arrangement look tired.

DISPLAY Arrange sunflowers in a large, spacious container. Umbel and spire shapes complement their daisy-shaped heads well. For foliage, I often include berried branches.

CARE If the leaves are removed and the water is topped up every 2 days, sunflowers can last for 7–10 days.

In the language of flowers,
tall sunflowers are a symbol of
haughtiness, while dwarf sunflowers
are a symbol of adoration.

Helianthus annuus is a giant,
annual species. This cultivar
is called 'Valentine'.

A Bucketful of Sunshine

I have fully embraced sunflowers' attention-seeking character by using two different varieties and making them the focal point of the arrangement. Their sunny colour is reflected by the other plants in the arrangement.

YOU WILL NEED

2 berried guelder
rose stems (Viburnum
opulus 'Roseum')

4 'Starburst Panache'
sunflowers (Helianthus
annuus 'Starburst
Panache')

15 'Valentine' sunflowers
(Helianthus annuus
'Valentine')

7 dill stems
(Anethum graveolens)

3 sweet clover stems
(Melilotus officinalis)

large enamel bucket

floral tack

2 plastic pinholders

block of floral foam

floral snips

ARRANGE

1 Using floral tack, stick two floral pin holders into the bottom of the bucket. Soak a block of floral foam in water and firmly press it onto the pin holders. Then fill the bucket with water.

2 Place the guelder rose stems so that they rest on the rim of the container, softening its edge. Cut the larger sunflowers ('Starburst Panache') so that they sit just above the foliage, and then anchor them into the floral foam.

3 Cut the remaining sunflowers at varying lengths so that they fill above and around the larger variety, before placing them into the arrangement.

4 Finish with the dill and sweet clover to soften and lift the heavy appearance of the sunflowers.

CARE

Top up the bucket with water every 2–3 days and keep it in a cool position. The arrangement will happily last for 7 days.

Mophead hydrangeas vary in colour
depending on the soil: acidic soil produces
blue flowers, and alkaline soil produces pink.

Hydrangea paniculata
'Grandiflora' *is a woody shrub*
with conical, lace-cap flower heads.

Hydrangea

Hydrangea

Hydrangeas' voluminous flowers change colour, ageing to beautiful antique shades.

The large, lush heads of hydrangea are in fact tree-like stem structures made up of hundreds of blossoms. While there are many types of hydrangea, two are most used for cutting: the mophead (*H. macrophylla*), which has rounded flower heads, and the lace-cap (particularly *H. paniculata*), which has smaller central flowers.

STEM HEIGHT
H. macrophylla, 1–2m (3–6½ft); *H. paniculata*, 3–7m (10–23ft), cut branches to desired length

FLOWER HEAD SIZE
H. macrophylla, 15–20cm (6–8in); *H. paniculata*, 7–20cm (2¾–8in)

LONGEVITY 5–7 days

FORMS mophead, lace-cap

COLOURS pink, purple, blue, yellow, orange, red, white

FRAGRANCE none

BEST COMPANIONS clematis, roses, zinnias

FROM THE FLORIST Choose a flower head with most of the florets open. The flower should feel sturdy and firm to the touch. Stems with older wood on which bark has formed are better for the conditioning stage as thay are able to take up water more efficiently.

IN THE GARDEN As woodland shrubs, hydrangeas prefer partial shade and shelter from wind and spring frosts. They like a moisture-retentive soil with plenty of organic matter, and will take 2–3 years to establish. Control the size of the flowers through pruning, and the flowers' colour through the acidity of the soil.

CONDITIONING Cut across and then up the stem vertically before searing (see pp.22–23). Place in deep water overnight to condition.

DISPLAY I prefer arranging the *H. paniculata* varieties with their lacy, cone-shaped flowers. The woody stems and neutral colours make them useful as framework material in bouquets, while their flower heads are a fantastic filler as they are both voluminous and airy and light.

CARE If the flowers start to wilt, recut the ends and re-sear. You can also try draping a cold, wet cloth over the flowers for around 4 hours.

Hydrangea Three Ways

I was inspired by three varieties of *Hydrangea paniculata* in all of their creamy green glory. These large, lacy, conical-shaped flowers form the core of this design.

YOU WILL NEED

2 hornbeam branches (Carpinus betulus)

2 eucalyptus stems (Eucalyptus parvifolia)

13 hydrangea stems (6 Hydrangea paniculata 'Grandiflora', 6 H. paniculata 'Limelight', 1 H. paniculata 'Pink Diamond')

2 zinnias (Zinnia 'Benary's Giant White')

2 leaved geranium stems (Pelargonium 'Chocolate Mint')

2 clematis (Clematis viticella 'Alba Luxurians')

3 meadow rue stems (Thalictrum delavayi 'Album')

4 tobacco plant stems (3 Nicotiana 'Lime Green', 1 N. langsdorffii 'Hot Chocolate')

metallic, footed bowl

secateurs

large, metal pinholder

floral tack

pot tape

ARRANGE

1 Tape a ball of chicken wire into the footed bowl. Fill the bowl with with water.

2 Position the hornbeam branches to create a triangular shape, with two branches horizontal and one vertical.

3 Cut the eucalyptus short and lay it on the front and sides of the vase's rim, so that it drapes over the sides of the bowl.

4 Start to fill the bowl with the hydrangeas, forming a low, mounded outline. Place the zinnias at the front, nestling them in between the hydrangeas.

5 Add the geranium stems, one at the front and one at the side, to create a diagonal of bright green across the arrangement. Balance this with the 'Lime Green' tobacco stems, dotting them through the hydrangeas to give an even spread of green.

6 Add the clematis, meadow rue, and remaining tobacco stems so they extend out of the hydrangeas. The clematis should trail down, and the meadow rue and tobacco stems reach upwards.

CARE

Hydrangeas have a much longer vase life in water than in floral foam, so this arrangement should last for 7 days if the water is topped up every 2–3 days.

Meadow rue

Zinnia

'Grandiflora'
hydrangea

Eucalyptus

Hornbeam

'Pink Diamond'
hydrangea

'Limelight'
hydrangea

Clematis

'Hot Chocolate'
tobacco plant

The addition of tobacco plant
and meadow's rue stems creates
an upper storey of delicacy.

'Lime Green'
tobacco plant

Geranium leaves

Hypericum
Hypericum

The glossy, perky hypericum berry is one of my favourite fillers for late summer and autumn.

Hypericum, or St John's wort, is covered with a profusion of small, bright yellow flowers in midsummer. But the plant's main event is the showier berries that follow the flowers in late summer. Clustered on branching woody stems, hypericum berries come in a range of colours. They are moderately poisonous, so should not be eaten.

STEM HEIGHT 1–2m (3–6½ft)

BERRY SIZE 5–10mm (¼–½in)

LONGEVITY 7–14 days

FORM clusters of berries

COLOURS green, yellow, orange, red, peach, cream

FRAGRANCE spicy

BEST COMPANIONS dahlias, zinnias, grasses

FROM THE FLORIST The berries should be firm and glossy, with healthy looking foliage.

IN THE GARDEN Hypericum will grow in partial shade or full sun. Prune right back in early spring to produce more strong, straight stems for cutting.

CONDITIONING Remove the lower leaves and cut the woody stems at a sharp angle before conditioning in water overnight.

DISPLAY Hypericum provides an interesting contrast of texture with its clusters of hard, shiny berries. The branching stems make an excellent filler in arrangements, and, because they are woody, support softer, less sturdy flowers in bouquets.

CARE Refresh the water every 2–3 days.

Hypericum x *inodorum* 'Magical Beauty' *is a hardy perennial with peach-coloured berries.*

Hypericum has long been used
as a treatment for mild depression,
and as a salve for cuts.

Limonium sinuatum '**Blue River**' *is a short-lived perennial with deep blue, papery bracts.*

Statice

Limonium

Despite its reputation as a dusty, dried flower, I love using statice as a fresh cut flower.

Statice is quite deceptive in its flowering. The branched stems are topped with what appear to be lots of small, papery, coloured flowers. However, these are actually calyces – a part of a plant that encloses the buds or petals. Statice's true flower is a smaller, white bloom that emerges from the centre of each of these structures.

Statice's botanical name, *Limonium*, is derived from the Greek word for meadow.

STEM HEIGHT
10–75cm (4–30in), depending on variety; *L. sinuatum*, to 40cm (16in)

FLOWER SIZE
0.5–1.5cm (¼–⅝in)

LONGEVITY 2 weeks as a fresh flower; longer if dried

FORM branched clusters of flowers

COLOURS purple, blue, yellow, peach, pink, white

FRAGRANCE none

BEST COMPANIONS
dahlias, roses, zinnias

FROM THE FLORIST Check that the true flowers have emerged, otherwise the stems will not last long once cut. Avoid calyces that are faded and slightly shrivelled. The stems and foliage are often a good indicator of freshness.

IN THE GARDEN Grow from seed directly or raise in a greenhouse and plant out in a sunny position after the last frost. Successional sowing will provide a continual supply of flowers from midsummer to the first frosts.

CONDITIONING Remove any of the winged growth on the stems that would fall below the water.

DISPLAY Statice lasts very well out of water, so I often use it in floral crowns and other hair flowers. It makes a wonderful filler in bouquets, and can be dried for wreath work.

CARE Change the water every 2–3 days.

Phlox

Phlox

Phlox's big, fluffy, cloud-like heads have a sweet, peppery fragrance.

Phlox flower heads are dense panicles made up of large florets. They come in an overwhelming range of varieties and colours. Many cultivars have a darker-coloured section in the centre of the florets, giving them a two-tone appearance. They are often at their best in mid- to late summer, when they are a welcome addition to the cutting garden.

STEM/BRANCH HEIGHT 15–150cm (½–5ft), depending on variety; *P. x arendsii*, to 1.5m (5ft)

FLORET SIZE 1–3cm (½–1¼in)

LONGEVITY 10 days

FORMS round or cone-shaped clusters of small flowers

COLOURS pink, purple, blue, red, white

FRAGRANCE sweet and peppery

BEST COMPANIONS roses, dahlias, sunflowers

FROM THE FLORIST Choose phlox with half of its florets open. Avoid those that are shedding florets.

IN THE GARDEN Phlox needs full sun or light shade and moisture-retentive soil. It is prone to fungal infection if it gets too dry, and needs lifting and dividing every 3 years to continue to flower well.

CONDITIONING Cut the stems at an angle and condition overnight in water before arranging.

DISPLAY Phlox do not have a strong form – they are rather irregular and "blobby". This means they are most useful as a filler between more defined shapes. Their colour and scent contribute beautifully to mixed compositions, and their large heads create volume for bold, statement pieces.

CARE Add floral preservative to the water to encourage the unopened buds to develop and open with good colour. Give the flower heads a shake every couple of days to dislodge any ageing flowers and make room for the buds behind to open.

In the language
of flowers, phlox
symbolize harmony.

***Phlox* x *arendsii* 'Utopia'** *is a*
large, highly scented variety with
lilac-pink flowers on tall stems.

Scabious

Scabiosa

Scabious's soft colour and simple, daisy-like form make it the perfect meadow-style flower.

The common name, pincushion flower, alludes to the central disk that houses the true flowers. These start as tight buds, giving the impression of lots of tiny pins packed tightly together. The annual variety, *S. atropurpurea*, has more of a dome-shaped flower head and comes in a wider range of colours.

STEM / BRANCH HEIGHT 20–90cm (8–36in), depending on variety; *S. caucasica*, to 90cm (36in)

FLOWER HEAD SIZE 4–8cm (1½–3in), depending on variety; *S. caucasica*, to 8cm (3in)

LONGEVITY 7–10 days

FORM flower head with domed central florets and larger outer florets

COLOURS purple, pink, red, blue, white

FRAGRANCE light and sweet

BEST COMPANIONS ammi, phlox, roses

FROM THE FLORIST The central florets should be tightly closed, and the outer petals open and looking clean and fresh.

IN THE GARDEN Scabious like an open, sunny position in well-drained, alkaline soil. The perennial variety (*S. caucasica*), will be short-lived if the soil gets waterlogged in winter. Keep picking and deadheading and it will flower for months. Sow the annual form (*S. atropurpurea*) in early autumn for much larger, more productive plants the following year. These should be supported with bean and pea netting stretched horizontally over the plants.

CONDITIONING Cut the stems at an angle and condition them overnight before arranging.

DISPLAY Their daisy-shaped flowers and long, wiry stems make scabious perfect for meadow-style arrangements. Use them as both a focal flower and a final flourish depending on their size and variety. The softer colours blend beautifully with blousy shapes for a romantic, English feel.

CARE Refresh the water every 2–3 days.

Scabious is rich in nectar and is known to attract pollinators.

Scabiosa caucasica *is a perennial variety with pale blue or lavender-blue flower heads.*

Wildflower Jar

I'm always drawn to a meadow-style when arranging scabious due to its wild nature. By using a selection of small-headed flowers without a dominant focal flower, you can conjure up something akin to a wildflower meadow. I decided to go for a soft, harmonious colour palette of lilacs, whites, and greens.

YOU WILL NEED

3 goat's rue stems
(Galega officinalis)

3 bellflower stems
(Campanula lactiflora)

15 scabious
(Scabiosa caucasica)

7 nigella stems (Nigella
hispanica 'African Bride')

3 tobacco plant stems
(Nicotiana langsdorfii)

5 yarrow stems (Achillea
'Summers Pastel')

5 bupleurum stems
(Bupleurum rotundifolium)

stoneware jar

floral snips

ARRANGE

1 Fill the jar with water. No support construction is necessary with this container as its neck is narrower than its bottom.

2 Cut and position the goat's rue stems first to form a framework. Keep the length long – two to three times the height of the container.

3 Add in the bellflowers next, cutting the stems to half the length of the goat's rue and using their frilly heads to fill in the lower section of the arrangement.

4 Fill any gaps with the scabious, nigella, tobacco, and yarrow. Hold them up to the arrangement to judge position and stem length, before cutting and placing. They should all be different heights and facing in different directions.

5 Finish with the bupleurum, which should be cut short and nestled in around the rim of the container.

CARE

This arrangement should last 7–10 days if the water is refreshed every 2–3 days.

In the language of flowers,
stonecrops are a symbol
of tranquillity.

Sedum 'Matrona' *is
a hardy perennial with bronze
leaves and purple stems topped
with soft, pink flowers.*

Stonecrop

Sedum

This garden classic provides a wonderful, textural finish to floral designs.

There are many stonecrop species. They tend to form sturdy clumps of thick, succulent stems topped with dense clusters of small, five-pointed, star-shaped flowers. These flat-topped clusters look just as beautiful in bud form as they do when the hundreds of tiny flowers open.

STEM HEIGHT
5–100cm (2–39in);
S. 'Matrona', 50–100cm (20–39in)

FLOWER HEAD SIZE
2.5–12cm (1–4¾in);
S. 'Matrona', 6–12cm (2½–4¾in)

LONGEVITY 10 days

FORMS flat clusters of small flowers

COLOURS pink, purple, blue, green, yellow, orange, red, white

FRAGRANCE none

BEST COMPANIONS dahlias, roses, snowberry

FROM THE FLORIST The stems and leaves should feel firm with their buds intact.

IN THE GARDEN Stonecrops are hardy, easy-to-grow perennials. They are drought tolerant and will happily grow in poor soil in full sun. To stagger their flowering period, cut back the stems by a third in late spring. They are easy to propagate by division in spring or autumn.

CONDITIONING Remove any leaves that would be under water and cut the stems at a sharp angle.

DISPLAY I prefer to use the flowers in their bud stage, when they are a useful, textural accompaniment to autumnal focal flowers and a wonderful contrast to grasses and berries. Use them to create a sturdy foundation for softer stems in hand-tied bouquets.

CARE Refresh the water every 2–3 days.

Snowberry was used by
Native Americans as an
antibiotic skin wash.

Snowberry

Symphoricarpos

Snowberry's pinkish white berries have a calming effect on vibrant autumnal hues.

My number one choice of autumnal, berried branches, snowberry produces generous clusters of berries along graceful, arching stems. The small, bell-shaped, pink flowers and the berries that follow are very popular with pollinating insects and birds. The berries can cause a stomach ache if ingested.

STEM HEIGHT 1–3m (3–10ft), depending on variety; C. Magical Series, to 1.2m (4ft)

FRUIT SIZE 0.5–1.5cm (¼–⅝in)

LONGEVITY 7 days

FORM branches of spherical berries

COLOURS red, pink, white

FRAGRANCE none

BEST COMPANIONS chrysanthemums, dahlias, roses, stonecrop

FROM THE FLORIST Ensure the berries are still firm and not dropping off of the stem.

IN THE GARDEN Snowberry is an easy-to-grow deciduous shrub. It is happy in most soil types, and will tolerate partial shade. In early spring, cut the stems back to allow long, straight new stems to grow the following season. Snowberry is extremely hardy and does not mind an exposed situation – I have used mine to create a cutting hedge that offers shelter to more fragile flowers.

CONDITIONING Cut across and then vertically up the woody stems with secateurs and place them in a deep bucket of water overnight.

DISPLAY I love mixing these softly coloured, berried branches with the last of my garden roses in the autumn. Their arching stems create an elegant outline in the vase, and they are a wonderful contrast to the richer, more sumptuous palette of autumn.

CARE Refresh the water and recut the ends of the stems every 2–3 days.

Symphoricarpos **'Charming Fantasy'** *is part of the* Magical Series, *a new line of snowberries being bred in the Netherlands for the cut-flower market.*

Strawflower

Xerochrysum bracteatum

Also called everlasting flower, strawflowers look like a cross between a pompon and a daisy.

Originally from Australia, strawflowers come in a range of vibrant colours. The petals are in fact bracts (specialized leaves) surrounding the tiny flowers in the centre of the flower head, which is produced on well-branched, tall stems. They attract pollinating insects and are excellent for drying.

STEM HEIGHT
10–100cm (4–39in), depending on variety; *X. bracteatum* Monostrum Series, to 90cm (36in)

FLOWER HEAD SIZE
1.5–8cm (⅝–3in), depending on variety; *X. bracteatum* Monostrum Series, to 8cm (3in)

LONGEVITY 7–10 days

FORMS single, double, fully double

COLOURS red, orange, yellow, pink, white

FRAGRANCE none

BEST COMPANIONS yarrow, hypericum, zinnias

FROM THE FLORIST Check the centres are still tight and there is no pollen. The leaves should be dark green with no signs of yellowing or decay.

IN THE GARDEN Strawflowers are hardy, easy-to-grow annuals that are both heat and drought tolerant. They will flower prolifically over a long period; this can be encouraged by regular picking and deadheading. Strawflowers can be raised in a greenhouse, but do well from a direct sowing in the spring. Tall plants may need support.

CONDITIONING Strip the lower leaves and cut the stems at a sharp angle before conditioning overnight.

DISPLAY Strawflowers make excellent dried flowers. If they are picked young and air dried, they retain their colour well. I like to use them as a final flourish where they can add a pop of colour to complement larger focal flowers. They are also excellent for buttonholes and hair flowers, lasting reliably out of water.

CARE Refresh the water every 2–3 days.

Strawflower's botanical name, *Xerochrysum* comes from the Greek words *xeros* meaning dry, and *chrysum* meaning golden.

Xerochrysum bracteatum
Monostrum Series *cultivars produce large, fully double flower heads in pink, red, orange, yellow, or white.*

Zinnia

— Zinnia —

The party animals of the cut-flower world, zinnias appear in a festive array of bright colours.

Zinnias are single or double, daisy-like flowers. Their brightly coloured, papery petals and intricate, jewel-like centres make them look almost artificial. There is a fantastic range of varieties available to cut-flower growers, from smaller, long-stemmed varieties to the bigger, dahlia-shaped types.

STEM/BRANCH HEIGHT 40–75cm (16–30in), depending on variety; *Z. elegans*, 60–75cm (24–30in)

FLOWER SIZE to 4.5cm (1¾in)

LONGEVITY 7–10 days

FORMS single, semi-double, double, fully double

COLOURS red, orange, yellow, pink, purple

FRAGRANCE none

BEST COMPANIONS dahlias, tobacco plants, dill

FROM THE FLORIST Choose flowers that are fully open, but display tight, clean centres with little pollen formation. The centre of the flower becomes more prominent as the flower ages.

IN THE GARDEN Zinnias love hot weather, so I grow mine under cover to guarantee a decent crop and a good stem length. Keep deadheading and picking them and the flowers will continue to replenish themselves from midsummer until the first frosts in autumn.

CONDITIONING Handle zinnias with care as they bruise easily. Condition them in water overnight in a cool room.

DISPLAY Zinnias are strong focal flowers – both in colour and form. They work well with acid-green foliage and fillers. For added texture and variety, I like to use berries, grasses, and seedheads with them.

CARE Refresh the water every 2–3 days.

In the language of flowers, zinnias are a symbol of affection for an absent friend.

Zinnia elegans **'Benary's Giant Coral'**
*is a fully double, annual form, meaning it
has more petals than single or double forms,
and only survives for one season.*

Collection of Colour

The clashing colours of zinnias work well
mixed together with greens in varying shades and
textures. To display as many colours and varieties as
possible I used a cluster of simple, cut-glass vases.

YOU WILL NEED

*24 zinnias of different
varieties (Zinnia elegans
'Benary's Giant Mix',
Z. elegans 'Sprite Mix',
Z. 'Jazzy mix')*

*4 sea holly flowers
(Eryngium x planum)*

*1 berried hypericum
stem (Hypericum
'Magical Beauty')*

*5 nasturtium stems
(Tropaeolum majus)*

*4 dill stems
(Anethum graveolens)*

*5 scented geranium
leaves (Pelargonium
'Lady Plymouth')*

*3 golden rod stems
(Solidago 'Ladsham')*

*3 tobacco plant stems
(Nicotiana langsdorfii)*

*4 quaking grass stems
(Briza maxima)*

5 small, cut-glass vases

floral snips

ARRANGE

1 Fill each vase with water and position them as you
want them to be displayed, arranging them in situ.

2 Cut the zinnias at varying lengths between one and
three times the height of the relevant vase, arranging
them so they all have plenty of space around them.

3 Add in the sea holly and hypericum, cutting them
short so they sit on the rim of the vases.

4 Fill any gaps in colour with the nasturtiums.

5 Finish with the dill, geranium leaves, golden rod,
tobacco, and quaking grass stems, creating some
vertical and horizontal interest to the collection.

CARE

Keep the small vases topped up with water every day
and the arrangement should last a week.

TROPICALS

Agapanthus

Agapanthus

Also known as African lily, agapanthus is an exotic beauty in stunning shades of blue or white.

Agapanthus flower heads are large, round umbels of trumpet-shaped flowers in shades of light blue to deep purple, and white. These magnificent heads sit upon strong, tall stems above lush, green, strap-like foliage. Originally from southern Africa, not all varieties are completely hardy.

The Greek word for love, *agape*, is part of agapanthus's botanical name.

STEM HEIGHT
0.6–1.5m (2–5ft)

FLOWER HEAD SIZE
10–20cm (4–8in)

LONGEVITY 2 weeks

FORMS rounded, intermediate, pendant

COLOURS purple, blue, white

FRAGRANCE none

BEST COMPANIONS
cosmos, larkspurs, roses

FROM THE FLORIST Choose stems on which the first flowers are beginning to open. Avoid those that have flowers that are drooping or facing downward.

IN THE GARDEN Agapanthus are sun lovers, so place them in full sun. Try to find a wind-sheltered position with well-drained soil as they dislike having wet roots during the winter. Protect their crowns in the winter with a good layer of compost. The clumps will gradually increase and can be divided after some years in the spring.

CONDITIONING Cut the stems at a sharp angle and condition in water overnight.

DISPLAY Keep the stems long for a bold, dramatic display where they are a focal flower – especially in the eye-catching blue shades. Alternatively, cut them short and work them into mixed compositions as a textural filler flower alongside blousy focal flowers.

CARE Remove spent florets by pinching them off. Keep the water clean by refreshing it every 2–3 days.

Agapanthus campanulatus
is a hardy variety with a rounded form.

African Lilies

I chose this vase to mirror the globe-shaped agapanthus. The subtle shades of this particular variety called for a sympathetic colour and the celadon glaze of this pot was the perfect match.

YOU WILL NEED

8 agapanthus (Agapanthus 'Headbourne White')

8 larkspur stems (Consolida ajacis 'Misty Lavender')

3 dahlias (Dahlia 'Eveline')

5 roses (Rosa 'Queen of Sweden')

5 dusty miller stems (Cineraria 'Silver Dust')

round, hand-thrown vase

chicken wire

floral snips

ARRANGE

1 Push a ball of chicken wire into the vase, then fill the vase with water.

2 Cut five of the agapanthus fairly short – around one-and-a-half times the height of the vase – and position them at a sharp angle so they nestle around the rim. Add in the last three at a slightly longer length – around twice the height of the vase – so that a domed outline is formed.

3 Break up the dome outline using the larkspur stems – they should be cut to two to three times the height of the vase. Fill in the gaps between the agapanthus with the dahlias and roses. Hold them up to the arrangement to judge position and stem length before cutting and placing.

4 Finish with the dusty miller, creating a collar of foliage to drape down the sides of the vase.

CARE

Top the water up every 2–3 days and the arrangement should last for 7 days.

Celosia

— Celosia —

Celosia's velvety flower head makes it an extraordinary and unique cut flower.

This opulent, striking flower comes in a beautiful range of luminous colours. Celosia is categorized into two groups: the Plumosa Group, with its plume-like flowers, and the Cristata or Cockscomb Group, which has crested flowers. Both offer a distinctive textural dimension to arrangements.

STEM HEIGHT
Cristata Group, 20–120cm (8–48in); Plumosa Group, 20–50cm (8–20in)

FLOWER SIZE
Cristata Group, 8–13cm (3–5in); Plumosa Group, 10–25cm (4–10in)

LONGEVITY 2 weeks

FORMS Cristata, Plumosa

COLOURS pink, red, orange, yellow, cream

FRAGRANCE none

BEST COMPANIONS hypericum berries, roses, zinnias

FROM THE FLORIST Check that the flowers have not been damaged by rough handling – the velvety frills are quite delicate and can bruise easily.

IN THE GARDEN Celosia requires hot, dry conditions to thrive. It is a half-hardy perennial that is grown as an annual. Sow indoors with heat, and then plant outside or under cover after the last frosts.

CONDITIONING Remove any excess foliage; then cut the stems at an angle, before placing them in clean water to condition overnight in a warm place.

DISPLAY Celosia's key addition to arrangements is its texture – I like to nestle it in amongst other flowers and foliage so that the frilly crests are seen.

CARE Keep the arrangement in a warm, well-ventilated environment as the flowers wilt more quickly when cold.

In Mexico, celosia is
known as *Flor de terciopelo*,
meaning "velvet flower".

Celosia argentea **var.** *cristata*
'Supercrest Mix' *is a large*
Cristata Group *variety.*

Jasminum officinale *is*
a deciduous, frost-hardy
variety known as common
jasmine or poet's jasmine.

Jasmine

Jasminum

This sweetly scented climber is smothered in white flowers during the summer months.

Each jasmine flower's petals are combined into a tube – spreading open at one end into a star shape. Its fine, pinnate foliage and twining stems make it equally useful as a decorative foliage material to add movement to floral designs. The sweet, heady fragrance is mainly produced by the buds rather than the flowers themselves.

STEM HEIGHT to 12m (39ft)

FLOWER SIZE 1–5cm (½–2in), depending on variety; *J. officinale*, to 5cm (2in)

LONGEVITY 5–7 days

FORMS single, semi-double

COLOURS pink, yellow, white

FRAGRANCE sweet, heady, and exotic

BEST COMPANIONS dahlias, roses, snowberry

FROM THE FLORIST Look for clusters with a few flowers already open.

IN THE GARDEN Jasmine enjoys a sunny, sheltered spot in the garden and is fairly drought tolerant, so does very well against a south facing wall. If happy, it will put on a lot of growth in a season and will need a lot of picking or pruning to keep it from taking over. When harvesting for foliage, wait until after flowering so that the stems are ripe enough to hold without wilting.

CONDITIONING Cut and sear the stems (see pp.23–24). Then condition them in water overnight.

DISPLAY I consider jasmine to be an excellent foliage plant. With its twisting, long stems it creates a beautiful wild outline to a bouquet or arrangement.

CARE The foliage will last longer than the flowers. Pull or pinch out the flowers when they shrivel or drop, and refresh the water every 2–3 days.

In the language of flowers, white jasmine is a symbol of amiability, and yellow jasmine a symbol of elegance.

Leucospermum cordifolium is a frost-tender, rounded shrub that produces solitary flower heads. This cultivar is called 'Succession'.

Pincushions' bright flower heads attract nectar-eating birds.

Pincushion

— Leucospermum —

Pincushions are instantly recognizable with their brightly coloured flower heads.

Pincushion's common name relates to its collection of arching styles, the brightly coloured structures that look like pins pushed into a pincushion. At the end of each style is a stigma, which is the pollen-bearing part of the plant. The tough, leathery leaves grow in a spiral formation around the stem.

STEM HEIGHT 2–4m (6½–13ft), depending on variety; *L. cordifolium*, to 2m (6½ft)

FLOWER HEAD SIZE 5–15cm (2–6in), depending on variety; *L. cordifolium*, 10–12cm (4–4¾in)

LONGEVITY 2 weeks

FORMS flower heads can be clustered or solitary

COLOURS yellow, orange, red, pink

FRAGRANCE none

BEST COMPANIONS ammi, celosia, hypericum berries

FROM THE FLORIST Check that the needle-like styles are all intact.

IN THE GARDEN These plants are indigenous to Zimbabwe and South Africa, and can only be grown elsewhere in controlled greenhouse conditions.

CONDITIONING Cut the woody stems at a sharp angle, remove any of the leaves that would fall under water, and condition overnight in water.

DISPLAY This is an unusual focal flower that works well with other tropical flowers and foliage. For a more informal garden style, it can also be mixed with roses, berries, grasses, and umbel-shaped flowers. The stems are very stiff and not particularly attractive, so I prefer to cut them short and hide them in amongst other flowers and foliage so that the only visible part is the flower head.

CARE Top up the water every 2–3 days and they will have a long vase life.

Red Heads

Although the soft green colour of the vase works really well for this arrangement, the narrow neck proved difficult with the stiff pincushion stems. To create some width, I used arching eucalyptus and ammi stems. The celosia and hypericum berries provide variation in texture and form.

YOU WILL NEED

5 eucalyptus stems (Eucalyptus parvifolia)

7 ammi stems (Ammi visnaga 'Green Mist')

10 pincushion stems (Leucospermum 'Succession')

5 celosia stems (Celosia argentea var. cristata)

5 berried hypericum stems (Hypericum 'Magical Pumpkin')

floral snips

large, hand-thrown, glazed vase with a narrow neck

ARRANGE

1 Fill the vase with water – because of its narrow neck, no extra support is needed.

2 Place the eucalyptus and ammi stems around the rim of the vase so that they create an arching outline.

3 Cut the pincushion stems to varying lengths between one-and-a-half and two-and-a-half times the height of the vase. Position the taller stems in the centre, angling out the shorter stems at the edges.

4 Work the celosia and hypericum stems in between the pincushion, nestling them in fairly low so that you cannot see the stems.

CARE

Top up the water every 2–3 days and the arrangement will last for 10 days.

Orchid

— Orchidaceae —

The diamonds of the cut-flower world, these exotic beauties are often reserved for special events.

There are thousands of varieties of orchid. The most commonly available as cut flowers are from the genera *Cymbidium*, *Dendrobium*, *Oncidium*, and *Phalaenopsis*. These come in every shade and colour except true blue. Orchids are usually multi-coloured, with spots or stripes accenting the centre of the flower, but single colour varieties are available.

STEM HEIGHT 15–100cm (6–39in), depending on variety

FLOWER SIZE 2–12cm (¾–4¾in), depending on variety

LONGEVITY 7–14 days

FORMS multiple, such as *Cymbidium*, *Dendrobium*, *Oncidium*, *Phalaenopsis*

COLOURS pink, purple, green, yellow, orange, red, white

FRAGRANCE none; *Cymbidium* varieties have a lemony scent with a touch of jasmine

BEST COMPANIONS roses, snowberry, grasses

FROM THE FLORIST Check that most of the flowers are open, as they may not open in the vase if they are cut too early in bud. Discoloured or wrinkled lower blossoms indicate the flowers are past their best.

IN THE GARDEN Orchids are primarily grown as a houseplant. The easiest variety to grow is *Phalaenopsis*, which needs indirect light and cool conditions. To water, place the plant in the sink and water for 15 seconds. Allow the plant to drain before returning to its original position.

CONDITIONING Cut 1cm (½in) off of the base of the stem while it is submerged in water, then condition in water overnight before arranging.

DISPLAY Orchids are versatile flowers to arrange, lending an exotic touch to any mixed composition. They have great lasting ability out of water, which is useful for bouquets and hair flowers in wedding work. I like to combine them with roses, berries, and grasses in late summer arrangements.

CARE Keep in a cool room and mist the flowers every day to prolong the vase life.

In the language of flowers, orchids are a symbol of refined beauty.

Phalaenopsis, or moth orchid, is one of the most elegant and easy-to-care-for indoor flowering plants.

Index

Penguin
Random
House

Editor
Toby Mann

Project Art Editor
Vicky Read

Pre-Production Producer
Robert Dunn

Producer
Ché Creasey

Jacket Designer
Harriet Yeomans

Jacket Co-ordinator
Libby Brown

Creative Technical Support
Tom Morse

Managing Editor
Dawn Henderson

Managing Art Editor
Marianne Markham

Art Director
Maxine Pedliham

Publishing Director
Mary-Clare Jerram

Photography
Gary Ombler and Clare West

First published in Great Britain in 2017 by
Dorling Kindersley Limited
80 Strand, London, WC2R 0RL

Copyright © 2017 Dorling Kindersley Limited
A Penguin Random House Company
2 4 6 8 10 9 7 5 3 1
001–280246–Feb/2017

A CIP catalogue record for this book is
available from the British Library.
ISBN 978-0-2412-2969-9

Printed and bound in China

A WORLD OF IDEAS:
SEE ALL THERE IS TO KNOW

www.dk.com

About the Author

Rachel Siegfried set up her flower farm Green & Gorgeous in 2008 and has been running it ever since. Located in the heart of the Oxfordshire countryside, Green & Gorgeous provides a local, seasonal, and natural alternative to more commercial suppliers. There, she and her partner Ashley grow seasonal flowers that she arranges for weddings and special events. They also run floristry and gardening courses for enthusiasts and professionals. Rachel imparts her distinctive, natural style on all of her arrangements, and considers her work an expression of her love for flowers.

Acknowledgments

Author's Acknowledgments

To my partner Ashley whose unrelenting support, hard work, and flexible skill set have in a large part made Green and Gorgeous the successful and thriving flower farm it is today. He takes up the slack and allows me to have the time and space to be creative with my flowers. Thank you to the rest of our team, twelve strong – a wonderful bunch who have all contributed to producing the flowers used in this book.

Additional thanks to Clare West for inspiring my floristry with her breathtaking photography; to Canadian-based potter Caroline Haurie for her beautiful hand-thrown, ash-glazed stoneware pot that I used for the opening chapter, and both the magnolia and lily arrangements; to Oxfordshire-based potter Harriet Coleridge for allowing me to use a range of her expertly thrown and glazed jugs, mugs, and footed vessels for the ranunculus, nigella, cosmos, and pincushion arrangements; and to Angelika at Flowervision London for helping me source the tropical flowers that are beyond my growing skills!

www.carolinehaurie.com
www.harrietcoleridge.co.uk
www.flowervision.co.uk

Publisher's Acknowledgments

DK would like to thank Sara Robin for photography art direction, Steve Crozier, Satish Gaur, and Sunil Sharma for retouching, Charlotte Chisholm for hand modelling, Jane Simmonds for proofreading, and Marie Lorimer for creating the index.

All images © Dorling Kindersley
For further information see: www.dkimages.com